Learn CS Concepts
with

Snap!

Create exciting games and animation in Snap and
learn Computer Science principles

Abhay B. Joshi

Book series on "Learning computer programming and CS principles"

To Sam Mahableshwerwalla, who inspired me like no one else

Published by:
Tanuja A. Joshi
3554 - 173rd CT NE
Redmond, WA 98052, USA
5 October 2018

Cover design by:
Ravindra Pande

To order your digital copy:
Go to Amazon.com

To order your printed copy:
Go to Amazon.com or write to: abjoshi@yahoo.com
Check pricing at: http://www.abhayjoshi.net/mybooks/bsnap.pdf

Other books in this series:
Learn CS Concepts with Scratch
Advanced Scratch Programming
Logo Programming Part 1 and 2
Pen Art in Scratch Programming

Click http://www.abhayjoshi.net/mybooks/csseries.pdf to see the complete list.

Preface

*The trouble with computers is you **play** with them. They are so wonderful. You have these switches - if it's an even number you do this, if it's an odd number you do that - and pretty soon you can do more and more elaborate things if you are clever enough, on one machine.*
- Richard P. Feynman, Theoretical Physicist

Background

"Snap!" is a programming language that is based on MIT's Scratch. You can run it in any web browser by using the link http://snap.berkeley.edu/run. In the subsequent discussion I am going to call it "Snap" (instead of "Snap!"). This book is an adaptation for Snap of my earlier book "Learn CS Concepts with Scratch". It is an introductory, self-study tutorial in which you will learn all these concepts through a series of exciting projects and programming activities.

The idea of using *computer programming as a medium for learning* is rapidly gaining acceptance. The benefits of learning programming and *computer science* concepts well before college – even in elementary grades – are well-understood.

Here is a list of some of the amazing things that happen when children engage in computer programming:

- Children become *active* and *creative* learners, because they explore ideas through a hands-on activity with an infinitely powerful tool.
- They learn to think about and analyze *their own thinking*, because that is the only way to program computers.
- They learn to solve complex problems by breaking them into smaller sub-problems.

- They learn a new way of thinking (called "computational" thinking).
- In the world of programming, answers are not simply "right" or "wrong"; this prepares a child's mindset for real-life problems.
- Children's learning processes are transformed from *acquiring facts* to *thinking creatively and analytically*.

About this interactive book

The choice of programming language is critical to achieve the intended objectives of teaching CS to beginners. In this book we use the Snap programming language. Snap is an entertaining and powerful language, and yet it is easy to learn. It is known as a "low floor and high ceiling" language – it allows the learner to build his/her vocabulary without getting mired in the complexities of syntax and grammar.

There is a lot of material on Snap Programming on the Internet, including videos, online courses, Snap projects, and so on. This book is meant to offer a more organized and tutorial-like treatment to learning Snap. It is also focused more on learning CS concepts rather than Snap itself.

Snap is a powerful language and offers access to lots of advanced ideas of Computer Science some of which are appropriate for a college-level programming course. We have not included these advanced ideas in this book since they certainly deserve a separate book for a serious treatment.

In short, this book is for students who are keen to learn CS concepts and have no prior programming background. We have only considered those features of Snap that are relevant to these introductory CS concepts.

I call this an "interactive book" because it is something between a traditional book – which is static and passive – and a fully interactive online course. It does look like a book: it has a series of chapters, diagrams, a lot of text, etc. But it also contains code snippets, references, which the reader is expected to explore to fully benefit from the ideas presented.

How the book is organized

The book is organized as a series of units – each containing a bunch of CS concepts and associated programming activities. Typically, each unit also includes a major programming project that helps you practice all the concepts learnt till then. Answers to all "review questions" and links to working programs for most of the programming exercises in the book are available online. Download them at: http://abhayjoshi.net/snap/book1/Solutions.pdf.

Additional Snap Material

The Internet is replete with study material, videos, and courses on Snap and Computer Science. I have listed below a few general Internet-based references that you could use to study Snap and CS concepts in more detail.

Snap website (snap.berkeley.edu):

This website is an authentic source of information related to Snap. Browse this website to access user guides, frequently asked questions, help with scripts, and video tutorials. The Snap manual in particular is an excellent reference:

https://snap.berkeley.edu/SnapManual.pdf

YouTube videos:

There are literally hundreds of YouTube videos that you can view to understand basic concepts of Snap. On the YouTube website, search for "Snap programming" to get a list of useful videos.

Pen Art in Scratch Programming by Joshi and Gaikwad

This book is distributed by Amazon.com. It is useful for units on pen commands and concepts related to "Pen art", such as recursion, to draw interesting and challenging geometric designs.

Hardware and Software

You can do all your Snap programming work online by creating your own account at http://snap.berkeley.edu.

Acknowledgements

I wish to thank Tanuja Joshi for reviewing the material of this book diligently and tirelessly and for providing me with valuable suggestions. I wish to thank Ravindra Pande for creating a truly beautiful cover for the book.

I wish to thank TEALS (https://www.tealsk12.org) – a nonprofit organization dedicated to the cause of teaching computer science to all high school students – for allowing me to teach Snap using their remote classroom infrastructure.

Finally, this book would not have been possible without the constant encouragement of my friends and family.

I do hope that you will find this book useful and enjoyable.

Abhay B. Joshi (abjoshi@yahoo.com)
Seattle, USA
5 October 2018

Author's background

As a freelance teacher (since 2008), Abhay's area of interest has been "teaching Computer Programming as a medium for learning" and he has been teaching Scratch regularly to elementary, middle, and high school students in Redmond and Bellevue, WA. He has also been teaching high school students at Aksharnandan School in Pune, India every summer since 2008.

Since 2011 Abhay has authored several books for a book series aimed at "Learning computer programming and CS principles". In 2011 he co-authored (with Sandesh Gaikwad) two books on Logo Programming and in early 2016 he authored two books on Scratch Programming. In 2017 he co-authored (with Sandesh Gaikwad) another book titled "Pen Art for Scratch Programmers". Abhay has written several articles to promote CS education, and has conducted teacher-training workshops to encourage aspiring teachers to experiment with this idea.

Abhay has been associated with the Software Industry since 1988 as a programmer, developer, entrepreneur, coach, and adviser. After getting an MS in Computer Engineering from Syracuse University (USA), he worked as a programmer for product companies that developed operating systems, network protocols, and secure software. In 1997, Abhay co-founded Disha Technologies, a successful software services organization.

Programming remains one of Abhay's favorite hobbies, and he continues to explore the "entertaining, intellectual, and educational" aspects of programming.

Anyone who has never made a mistake
has never tried anything new.

Albert Einstein

Contents

Unit 0: Introduction

Cauliflower is nothing but cabbage with a college education.
- Mark Twain

In this book, in addition to learning a lot of Computer Science concepts, you will do a series of interesting projects and programming activities. You don't need to have any prior programming experience or expertise for this course. This is supposed to be your first encounter with computer programming.

You might ask: Why should I learn CS concepts and Snap? Why should I bother learning computer programming at all?

The fact is every one of us today works with computers. Your smartphone is a computer which you use for communication and games and so many other things. When you go online to do shopping or to find information you are using computers. When you go to a grocery store the person at the checkout counter is using a computer to scan your items. Your car most likely has a computer to control certain things like the inside temperature.

But, in all these cases we are working with the computer as "consumers" or "users". Someone else – people called "programmers" – at companies such as Microsoft or Google or Cisco created all those services that we use.

I think it is much more exciting to engage with computers as creators, as designers. Can we not ask the computer to do things for us, things which are not already made by someone else? Programming is the new kind of magic that will allow you to be a modern-day wizard. And that is what is meant by "Creative Computing" – designing and creating things using programming.

By the way, there is another great reason to learn computer programming. Practically all future careers will use computers, and so, if you are armed with the power of programming, you will have an edge in your career!

Ok, so, what tool should we use to do creative computing? For this course the tool we are going to use is a language called Snap. Snap is an exciting environment in which we can design all kinds of cool stuff – animation, games, interactive art, science experiments, and so on. Snap is freely available to anyone, and it was developed at UC Berkeley.

A few simple guidelines:

As I said earlier, you will do a lot of programming in this course. You will work on a few big projects, and you will also write many small "practice programs".

You will learn and apply concepts of computer programming and computer science when you write these programs. So, work on every program sincerely. Give your best and do not hesitate to ask me questions via email.

Learning programming is just like learning a new sport. The more you practice the better you get at it. Also, you learn when you make mistakes. So, don't feel bad when your programs don't work. In fact, feel happy when they don't work! Because that is how you will learn more.

For this course you should maintain a design notebook. I recommend that you use Microsoft PowerPoint or Word for this purpose. But, if you don't have or know any of these, feel free to use any other word processor or even Notepad. Use the design notebook not only to answer the review questions, but also to make notes of points that you think are important and interesting.

All right! We will now open up Snap and understand its user interface.

Unit 1: Short Story Animation

If you want to be creative, stay in part a child, with the creativity and invention that characterizes children before they are deformed by adult society. – Jean Piaget

Concepts learnt in this Unit

- Snap User Interface
- Paint editor
- Sequence
- Motion commands
- Simple looping (repeat, forever)
- Absolute motion
- Relative motion
- Smooth motion using repeat
- Nested looping
- XY geometry
- Costume-based animation
- Multiple backdrops
- 3-D effect using looping
- Basic sound commands
- Synchronization using broadcasting

Chapter 1.1: First Look at Snap

Snap UI:

Connect to your Snap account at http://snap.berkeley.edu and get familiar with its basic interface. The following figure points out some of the main parts of the Snap interface.

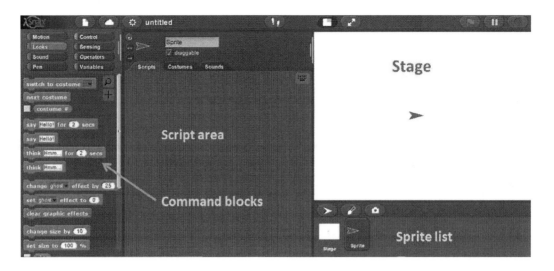

When you start Snap this is how it looks. It's a bit like a movie maker's studio. You are the movie director and your characters do things according to your instructions.

The white area is called the "stage". That's where all the action happens. Whatever you tell your characters to do they do it on that stage.

Your characters are called "sprites". They are all lined up in the area below the stage.

Now, as you might know, in a movie or a play each character follows a script. Similarly in Snap every sprite has a script associated with it. You, as the programmer, have to create that script. The "script area" in the above figure is where the sprite's script appears.

How do you build a script? You build a script using the command blocks listed at the left. There are various types of command blocks: motion, control, sound, etc. You drag and drop these blocks into the script area and connect them together (like jigsaw pieces) to build a script.

You can save your Snap project in two ways: First, you can save it in your cloud account provided by Snap (see File->Save or File->Save as). Or you can save it locally (on your computer) by using the "Export project" feature in the File menu. This feature exports your project to XML format.

Sprites and costumes:

Every character that will take part in your Snap project is called a sprite. The following image shows ways in which you can add new sprites to your project. When you add a new sprite it always comes up as a "Turtle" (the triangle-like shape). Every new Turtle sprite appears at a random place on the screen, facing a random direction, and has a random color.

You can then change the appearance of your sprite, by loading a new costume. There are multiple ways of loading a new costume. First, you can choose from Snap's own collection of hundreds of readymade costumes. There are animals, people, fantasy characters, cars, planes, and so on. To add a costume to your sprite from this Snap library, first click the costumes tab as shown below.

And then click the File menu to load the Costumes library as shown below:

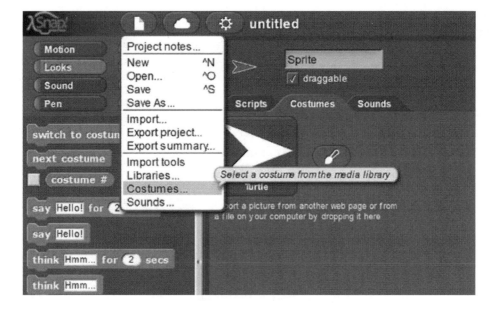

Secondly, you can paint your own costume by using the built-in paint editor of Snap. Click on the paint icon to start the Paint editor and draw the new costume. If you have used Microsoft Paint or some other similar drawing software, you will find this Snap Paint Editor very easy to use.

Tip: You can also *modify* an existing costume using this paint editor.

Finally, you can import an image from your computer and use it as a costume. Use the "Import" menu item of Snap, or simply drag and drop the image file on to the costumes tab.

Stage or background:

Similar to the costume library for sprites, Snap comes with a lot of interesting backgrounds which you can load for your stage. If you want to use one of those, click on the File menu and then on the "backgrounds" menu item.

If you want to draw your own background, click on the little paint icon. You will once again see the Paint editor interface.

Tip: You can also *modify* an existing backdrop using this paint editor.

You can also import an image from your computer and use it as a background. Use the "Import" menu item of Snap, or simply drag and drop the image file on to the backgrounds tab of your Snap project.

Command blocks and Scripts:

In the leftmost pane of the Snap UI you will see a list of command blocks such as:

There are several categories (or palettes) of commands, such as "Motion", "Looks", "Sound", and so on. We will learn about these various command blocks throughout this book.

Every sprite has its own program(s) called script(s). You can create a script by snapping together command blocks.

If you want to simply check out what a particular command block does before using it in a script, you can just click on that command block (without dragging it to the script area). For example, we have this command block . If you click on it the sprite will turn by 15 degrees.

Once you build a script, you can click on it to run it. For example, this script below asks the sprite to move, take a turn, and move again.

When a script is running, a white glow appears around it. That tells us that that script is running. For example, in the script below the sprite turns around itself forever. When we click on it the white glow appears around it.

To stop a running script, click on it again. The white glow disappears and the script stops running.

Review questions:

1. Snap allows you to use your own image/picture when you draw a new sprite. True or False?

2. What is "Snap"?
   a. It is a computer programming language
   b. It is a software (like Photoshop) in which you can create graphics and animation
   c. It is a type of computer system like Windows or Linux
   d. It is a collection of readymade animations and video games

3. See the script below:

   This script will run when
   a. You click on the Green Flag
   b. You press the ENTER key
   c. You click on the script
   d. You click on the sprite

4. What is the difference between the two following commands?

Programming practice:

Experiment with the following command blocks and create your own scripts.

Chapter 1.2: Sequence and Sounds

Build a script as shown below and play with it. Understand the sequence of operations.

```
say Hello! for 2 secs
say How are you guys? for 2 secs
think Hmm...what should I show them? for 2 secs
say See, I can move! for 2 secs
move 100 steps
say I can change color too! for 2 secs
change color effect by 25
say Now, I am going to hide ... for 2 secs
hide
wait 2 secs
```

Next, build the following script and play with it:

```
show
say Hi again!!! for 2 secs
say Watch me grow big ... for 2 secs
wait 1 secs
change size by 50
say Now, just watch! for 2 secs
turn 90 degrees
wait 1 secs
move 100 steps
wait 1 secs
turn 90 degrees
```

Next, build the following script and run it.

```
say  Ok, it's time to go home ...  for  2  secs
go  to  x:  0  y:  0
point  in  direction  90 ▼
set  size  to  100  %
```

Finally, connect the three scripts all together, and run the whole program together.

Do you have some understanding now of these different command blocks and how scripts are built in Snap? In this exercise, we learnt the *Sequence* concept as summarized below.

Sequence:

Snap programs tell the computer precisely what to do, step-by-step. To create a program in Snap, you need to think about the order of steps. Unlike humans, computer programs do not change the order of the commands given to it.

For example, let's say you were given a "To do" list as follows:
1. Get clothes from the laundry
2. Check mail in the post office box
3. Buy grocery

You may not follow this task-list exactly in the given order. You might go to the grocery shop first, or even skip getting the mail.

Computers do not have this freedom. They would, if given the above list, follow it exactly in the given order, one after the other, making sure every item was completed in a satisfactory manner before going to the next. This concept is called "Sequence" in computer science.

Here is an example of a Snap script that demonstrates the concept of sequence. The color will change at the very end of the program. The sprite will jump to the center of screen first. And so on.

Playing sounds:

One of the exciting features of Snap is the ability to play sounds.

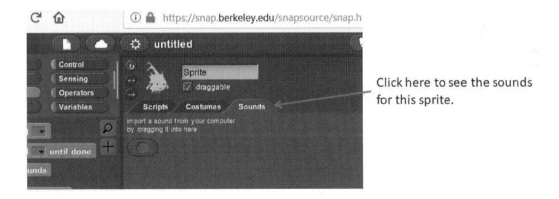

Click here to see the sounds for this sprite.

As shown above, every sprite has a tab called "Sounds". Under this tab, you need to collect the sounds that you would like to play in your program. You can import an existing sound from the Snap library (by clicking "File" and then "Sounds"). You can also import your own sound file in MP3 format by dragging and dropping it in this area. Finally, the red button allows you to record your own sounds if your computer is equipped with a microphone.

Once you create a list of sounds for a sprite, you can play these sounds using the following sound commands. We have imported a sound called "Cat".

This command waits until the entire sound file has been played and only then moves to the next command in your script.

On the other hand, this command starts playing the sound and then immediately moves to the next command in your script. This is useful if you want to play a sound as background score.

This command stops all sounds that might be playing at that time.

Review questions:

1. How many times will you hear "Cat" sound when you run the script below?

2. How many times will you hear "Cat" sound when you run the script below?

3. We've created the following program for our sprite. What will it do when we click this script?

    a) It will move, wait for 1 second and then meow.
    b) It will move and meow at the same time.
    c) It will not do anything.
    d) It will meow, wait for 1 second and then move.

Programming practice:

1. Write a script which when clicked does the following. Each action must be visible separately (so you may have to insert the "wait" command).
   - The sprite will greet you and tell its name.
   - It will walk 100 steps and then grow in size.
   - It will jump to x=-100 and y=-100. It will then shrink in size.
   - It will say "Hey I am down here!"
   - It will bid farewell with a sound and hide.

2. When clicked your program should play a composition (sequence of notes).

Chapter 1.3: Green flag, Looping, and Costumes

We will now do a programming activity in which there are two sprites. Pick two sprites and load any costumes for them from the Snap library. In my program, I have taken Alonzo and a space ranger robot.

Create the following scripts for the two sprites:

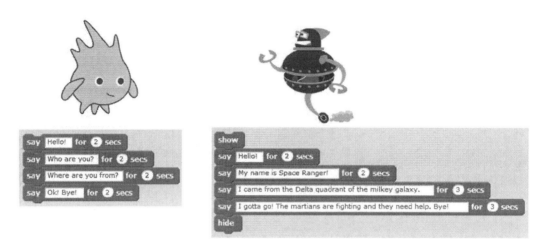

The main problem you will notice is that there is no way to run both these scripts at the same time. You can only click one script at a time.

Green Flag:

This is where the following green flag "hat" block comes in handy.

Just attach this block on top of each of the above scripts as shown below:

Now, if you click the Green flag at the upper right corner of the Snap interface (as shown below), you will see that both these scripts start at the same time.

Green flag

But, things are still not quite right. The two characters speak at the same time, without pausing for each other.

That is a problem with your scripts, not with Snap. The pauses must be built into the scripts, just like in real life we pause when conversing with someone. See the addition of "wait" commands in the modified scripts below.

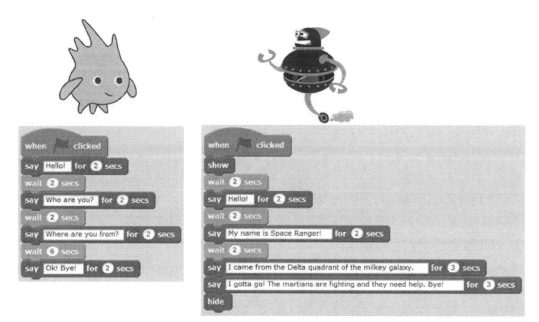

If you click on the Green flag now, you will observe a proper conversation between the two characters.

Next, we will learn the concept of looping.

Simple looping (repeat, forever):

Looping (also known as *iteration*) is the repetition of a sequence of commands. The "repeat" and "forever" commands in Snap allow simple looping:

The sprite will move in a square.

The sprite will spin around itself forever.

In order to use looping effectively, it is essential to first get the basic sequence working properly.

For example, let's say we want a sprite to jump up and down repeatedly. We should first get the basic command sequence, i.e. one jump, working properly as shown below:

Jumping involves moving up and down. So, just using two different values for "y" should do the trick.

Now, making 4 jumps is a simple matter of putting this sequence inside a REPEAT block:

Smooth motion using repeat:

Let's take an example in which we will see an interesting use of REPEAT.

Place your sprite somewhere near the left edge and click the following script.

The sprite will jump to the right by 300 steps. It seems as if the jump was instantaneous. Indeed, most Snap commands take an extremely short time to run. Looping can, in fact, reveal that these commands are not really instantaneous. Run the following modified script:

The sprite goes the same distance (10x30 = 300) but a bit more smoothly. That's because the extremely short but *finite* time taken by each "move" adds up 10 times. (Note that the time taken by "move" is the same irrespective of its input, i.e. the # of steps.)

Now, try the following script:

Once again, the sprite goes the same distance (30x10 = 300) but it goes smoothly at a slower speed.

So, there you have it! You can use REPEAT to create smooth motion, and the speed of the motion depends on the size of each step.

The same principle applies to rotation (spinning). The following two scripts spin the sprite but at different speeds.

Faster

Slower

What if you wanted your sprite to just walk horizontally (east-west) forever? See the following script:

Note the "if on edge, bounce" command. It ensures that the sprite doesn't go past the screen edges. See the screen-shot below to understand how to control the sprite's orientation after bouncing.

Rotation style:

The yellow box highlights 3 buttons that control how the sprite will behave when it bounces on edges (or turns). Click the one that meets your needs.

The first button indicates free rotation, and it will cause the sprite to become upside-down after bouncing off an edge.

The second button indicates left-right orientation, and it will cause the sprite to only face either left or right after bouncing off an edge.

The third button indicates no rotation, and it will cause the sprite to always face right (or East) no matter where it bounces or how much it turns.

Animation using costumes:

Animation, as you know, is an illusion of action or motion. We can make pictures of people, animals, and even of inanimate objects appear alive by making them do things.

Motion is one way to create animation. But, there is one shortcoming in that. Motion commands make the whole sprite move. You cannot move its parts. There is no hand-waving or change of expression or anything like that.

Animation is basically a trick played on our eyes. When we see a succession of slightly changing pictures rapidly one after the other, for example, the pictures of a hand moving up, our eyes think that we actually saw a hand moving up!

In Snap this series of pictures is called costumes. Every sprite can line up its costumes in the "Costumes" tab. We have discussed how to load costumes in an earlier section on "Sprites and costumes".

Once you line up the costumes, you use the following commands to actually use these costumes to create animation.

The "next costume" command will make the sprite change its appearance and look like the next costume in its list of costumes. When it reaches the end of the list it goes back to the first costume in the list. (Note: The original "turtle" costume is not used by this command.)

The command "switch to costume" allows the sprite to change to any costume in the list. This is handy when you don't have an orderly series of costumes, but a set of costumes that your sprite wants to use in no particular order.

Let's take an example. Let's say we have lined up costumes as shown below:

Now, create the following scripts and see what happens when you press the SPACE key again and again.

Do you see Avery actually walking (and not just dragging her feet)?

Can you now make Avery walk back and forth continuously? See the following script:

The "wait" command helps to make the animation a bit more realistic.

Multiple backdrops:

The Snap stage can have multiple backdrops. There are a number of ways to create a new backdrop:
- Choose from the Snap library
- Paint using the paint editor
- Upload an image from your computer

Once you have lined up multiple backdrops for the stage, the stage can change the backdrop any time using the same costume commands (listed under the "Looks" tab) as we have seen above.

Review questions:

1. Let's say you have painted a new penguin sprite. When you run the command "point in direction 90" on the penguin sprite, the penguin looks left instead of right. What is the problem?
    a. Direction 90 means the left direction
    b. You painted the original image of the penguin to look left
    c. There is a bug in the script
    d. The center of the sprite is not correct

2. What is the distance covered in the script shown below?

    a. 5 steps
    b. 20 steps
    c. 25 steps
    d. 100 steps

3. To make your animation look realistic you should have as many costumes as possible. True or False?

Programming practice:

1. From the Snap library load a sprite that has flying costumes (e.g. bat or parrot). Write a script to make the sprite change costume each time the space bar is pressed. Add code so that the sprite will face to the left, move a few steps and also change costume when the left arrow key is pressed. So, it should look as if the sprite is flying west each time you press left arrow key.

2. You can make the "Avery" sprite walk by using the "next costume" command as shown below. Do the same using the "switch to costume" command.

3. Use existing costumes (in the Snap library) to create animation, such as, a walking boy or a fire-breathing dragon.

4. Draw your own costumes using the Paint editor.

Chapter 1.4: XY Geometry and Motion

Using the motion commands in Snap you can create all kinds of interesting motion. First let us understand the layout of the Snap stage and how several motion commands make use of it.

XY Geometry:

We use the screen in Snap as a geometric plane. Every point on the screen has X and Y coordinates. You might have learnt about this in your school mathematics.

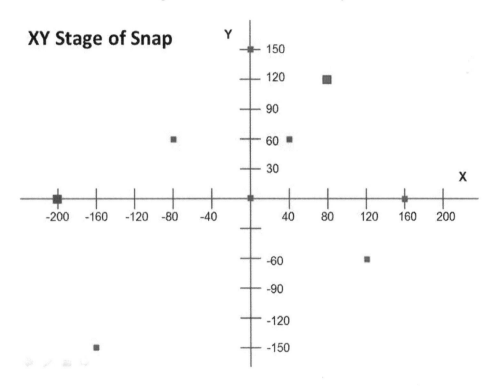

Every point on the screen has two coordinates: x and y. Imagine two number lines laid out on the screen: one horizontally and the other vertically, both intersecting at 0. The horizontal line is called the X axis, and the vertical line is called the Y axis. The distance of a point from the Y axis is called the X coordinate, and the distance from the X axis is called the Y coordinate.

For example, for the blue point here its distance from the Y axis is 80, so its X coordinate is 80. And its distance from the X axis is 120, so its Y coordinate is 120.

For the dark red point its distance from the Y axis is -200, so its X value is -200. And its distance from the X axis is 0, so its Y coordinate is 0.

Every sprite in Snap has a center point which you can view (and change) in the Paint editor. The X Y coordinates of this center point are assumed to be the X Y coordinates of the sprite. When the sprite moves these values also change automatically.

How do you find out the X and Y values of a particular location on the screen? You can use the following *reporter* blocks for this purpose. Look under the "Motion" category just below "if on edge bounce". (We will discuss *reporters* in greater detail later.)

Turn these reporters on (i.e. check the little boxes next to them), and they will report the current X and Y values of your sprite. If you move the sprite to a different location, the reporters will indicate the new X and Y values.

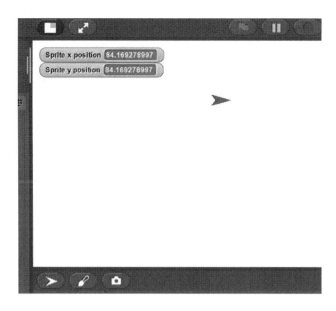

Now that we understand what X Y coordinates are let us look at a few Snap commands that make use of these coordinates.

The Go To command makes the sprite jump to a specific point on the screen. The jump is instant, not a smooth one.

The Glide command makes the sprite move smoothly to another point. The sprite's speed depends on the number of seconds.

These commands will move the sprite only left and right because its Y coordinate will remain the same.

These commands will move the sprite only up and down because its X coordinate will remain the same. So you could use these commands to make a sprite jump up or down.

The SET commands are interesting because they move the sprite to a specific point no matter where the sprite is right now; whereas, the CHANGE command depends on the sprite's current location.

For example, if you say "CHANGE X by 10" the sprite will move to its right by 10 pixels. If you run "CHANGE X by 10" once more, the sprite will again move to its right by 10 pixels.

But, if you say "SET X to 100", the sprite will jump to where X is 100. And if you run "SET X to 100" once more, nothing will happen because the sprite is already at X = 100.

There is one important thing to note about all these commands shown here. The orientation, or, the direction in which the sprite is facing, does not change when you use any of these commands.

Orientation of a sprite is basically the direction in which it is facing. It is shown in terms of the angle made with the North direction. So if a sprite is facing North its direction value is 0.

Initially all sprites are facing east, which means their direction is 90. You can change a sprite's orientation using one of the commands shown below.

The TURN commands turn the sprite around its center point either clockwise or anti-clockwise.

This command makes the sprite face in any direction you want. You can pick one from the drop-down list, or you can enter a value of the angle.

Nested looping:

Nesting means having one loop inside another. See the example below:

The following script makes the sprite jump up and down. Repeat makes the jump appear smooth.

What if we wanted the sprite to jump 5 times?

The two inside repeat loops together make the sprite jump once, and the outside loop makes the jump happen 5 times. Thus, nesting of loops can open up interesting opportunities.

Review questions:

1. A sprite has a script as shown below:

When you click on the Green flag:

a. The sprite will move 100 steps
b. The sprite will move forever
c. The sprite will move 1 step
d. The sprite will move 100 steps and turn 100 degrees

2. As a sprite moves up, its X-value ...
    a. Gets bigger
    b. Get smaller
    c. Stays the same

3. How do you make a sprite jump up and down?
    a. Use a pair of "Glide" commands
    b. Use a pair of "go to x, y" commands
    c. Use the "change y" command in a pair of Repeat blocks
    d. All of the above

Programming practice:

Note: Look up http://abhayjoshi.net/snap/book1/videos.htm to check out videos of sample solutions.

1. Write a "commotion" program in which various animals are made to perform different actions, such as:
    o   constantly jumping up and down
    o   spinning around itself
    o   roaming around the screenetc.

Chapter 1.5: Animation Mini-project

This is a mini-project assignment for you, in which you will apply all the concepts and commands learnt so far. The specification of this project is as follows:

Specification: About-me or Monologue

In this project you have two options: (1) Make a story of yourself (and your friends and family) or (2) Design a monologue.

- **About-me**: One primary sprite (for you) and other sprites (friends and family). In the animation you (i.e. the sprite representing you) talk about yourself – your name, family, house, hobbies, etc. Other sprites don't say anything or perform any actions.
- **Monologue**: Similar to "about-me" except the sprite will make up its own story.

Project Requirements:

- Green flag should start the animation.
- Only 1 active sprite.
- Use as many commands learnt so far as possible (movement, rotation, etc.).
- Use sounds and costumes.

Note: Look up http://abhayjoshi.net/snap/book1/videos.htm to check out videos of sample solutions.

Chapter 1.6: More Motion and Broadcasting

Absolute motion:

Absolute motion refers to motion whose result *does not* depend on your current position and direction. For example, "Going to Washington DC" is absolute motion because you will end up in Washington DC no matter where you currently are.

The following Snap commands (among others) describe absolute motion because the resulting position or direction *does not* depend on the sprite's previous position or direction.

Relative motion:

In contrast to absolute motion, relative motion depends on your current position and direction. For example, "Turn right" is relative motion because the resulting direction depends on your current direction.

The following Snap commands (among others) describe relative motion because the resulting position or direction *does* depend on the sprite's previous position or direction.

3-D effect using looping:

Everything in Snap – sprites and backgrounds – is 2-D (two dimensional). You can't make a sprite turn around and face away from you (unless of course you have a suitable costume). But there is a bit of 3-D that you can achieve with the use of repetition and change of size. When a sprite moves away from you, its size shrinks. Conversely, if you decrease its size it will appear as if it is moving away. The same principle applies to growing and increasing the size.

Load the costumes "Dove 1" and "Dove 2" and load any outdoor background. Create and run the following script. What do you see?

Do you see a bird flying towards you?

Synchronization using broadcasting:

When you write a program that contains multiple sprites that interact with each other in some way, you need to worry about synchronization – which basically means proper coordination of their actions.

To understand synchronization, let us look at an example, as shown above. Here, we have two sprites – Alonzo (he calls himself Gobo) and Space Ranger – talking with each other. If you run the program what will happen? They both will talk at the same time! There is no proper sequence or coordination. That's not what you expect, right? To make it a proper dialog, Alonzo should say "Hi" first, then, the space ranger should reply by saying "Hello", and so on.

So we say that there is no *synchronization* in this program. Do you now see the meaning of synchronization? We have already seen one way to fix this problem – by inserting "wait" statements. Let's now learn about a much more elegant technique called "Broadcasting".

You might have heard the word "Broadcasting" in the context of radio and TV. When you tune into a radio station, you are actually listening to something that was broadcast from a radio station.

Broadcasting basically means sending a message to anyone who cares to listen. So, when someone gives a public speech, he/she is giving a *broadcast* speech.

In Snap, broadcasting has a similar meaning. When you use the BROADCAST command (under the "Control" tab), your sprite sends a message that goes to every sprite in your program and even to the stage.

But, just like not everyone is interested in listening to the radio, not every sprite may be interested in hearing the message. So, if a sprite is interested in receiving that message it uses the command WHEN I RECEIVE. So, in effect, broadcasting can also be used to pass messages one-to-one, i.e. between two entities.

So here are all the commands related to broadcasting:

WHEN I RECEIVE is an event and works just like other hat blocks. When the specified message is received, the script attached underneath it runs.

Every time the exact same message is received the script runs again.

There are two flavors of the BROADCAST command as shown above:

In the first flavor, the sending sprite sends the broadcast message and immediately goes to the next command in the script, if there is any.

But, in the second flavor, the sending sprite sends the broadcast message and waits – until all listening sprites have received the message and completely run each of their "WHEN I RECEIVE" scripts.

Example:

To understand the difference between these two broadcasts, run the following experiment:

Take any two sprites sprite1 and sprite2. Create the following script for sprite1:

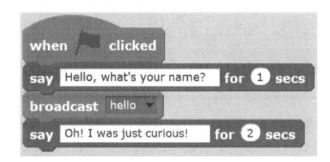

Create the following script for sprite2:

And now run the program by clicking on Green Flag. Observe the conversation. You will notice that it doesn't look right. Now, replace the "broadcast" command in sprite1's script by "broadcast and wait". Run the program again by clicking the Green Flag.

Review questions:

1. The Snap command "point in direction" causes relative motion. True or False?

2. If you run the command, the new position of the sprite on the screen depends on the current position.
   a) True
   b) False

3. We have two sprites sprite1 and sprite2. They have scripts as shown below:

Script for sprite 1   Script for sprite 2

What will happen when the green flag is clicked?
   a) Sprite1 will say "I asked him to run".
   b) Sprite2 will stop running after 2 seconds because the STOP command will stop the program after 2 seconds.
   c) Sprite1 will never say anything.
   d) The results will be unpredictable.

4. In a particular game program, sprite1 is supposed to send a "GO" signal to all sprites so that they can start doing their work, and then sprite1 is supposed to count time. Which of the following commands should sprite1 use to send the "GO" signal?

B1:

B2:
   a) Sprite1 should use command B1
   b) Sprite1 should use command B2
   c) Sprite1 should first use B1 and then B2
   d) Sprite1 should first use B2 and then B1

5. Let's say we have two sprites Kitty and Abby. Their respective scripts are shown below.

Script for Kitty   **Script for Abby**

What will happen if you click on one of these scripts?

    a. Nothing happens - this doesn't work because there is a loop.
    b. Kitty and Abby will keep saying "Hello" to each other until you hit the red stop button.
    c. Kitty and Abby will say "Hello" to each other only once.
    d. Kitty and Abby will say "Hello" to each other simultaneously.

Programming practice:

Note: Look up http://abhayjoshi.net/snap/book1/videos.htm to check out videos of sample solutions.

1. Write a "circus" program in which the ringmaster calls animals/actors one by one and each performs some act.

2. Write a "roll call" program in which the teacher calls students one by one and each says "present" if present. Show one or two as being absent – someone else will inform the teacher.

Chapter 1.7: Project Animation

This is a project assignment for you, in which you will apply all the concepts and commands learnt so far. The specification of this project is as follows:

Specification: Short story

In this project you will design a short story animation. This can be a nursery rhyme, a folk story, your own story, or a clip from your favorite story. The story should be narrated as sub-titles or as part of the animation.

Project Requirements:

- Green flag should start the animation.
- At least 2 sprites.
- Draw at least one background.
- Use as many commands learnt so far as possible (movement, rotation, broadcasting, etc.).
- Use sounds and costumes.
- Sprite names must be as per the story, and not sprite1, sprite2, etc.
- As each line of the story appears on the screen (anywhere) animation of that line should be visible.
- Story should be slow and easy to understand.
- It should take at least 10 seconds but not more than a minute.

Note: Look up http://abhayjoshi.net/snap/book1/videos.htm to check out videos of sample solutions.

Write in your Design book:

- A short description of your project
- Answer these questions:
  1. What did you learn?
  2. What was exciting?
  3. What was challenging?

Abhay B. Joshi

Unit 2: Fly a Helicopter

Show a kid how to play a game, you have changed his day! Show him how to program a game, you have changed his life! - Abhay Joshi

Concepts learnt in this Unit

- Events
- Reset script
- Graphic effects
- Concurrency
- User interaction using keyboard
- Conditions: YES/NO questions
- Sensing touch
- Conditionals (IF)
- Conditionals (IF-Else)
- Stopping scripts

Chapter 2.1: Events, Reset Scripts, Concurrency

While working on your first project (of the previous unit) you might have noticed one problem. At the end of the program, you have to manually bring all sprites back to where they are supposed to be at the beginning and change their appearance back to what it was. Otherwise, the next time you run the program, it doesn't work properly. To avoid this manual work, you can make use of an idea called "Reset script".

But, before we understand how to write reset scripts, let's understand the concept of events.

Events:

Events are outside happenings that create some sort of a signal. For example, the "ringing of a phone" is an event that tells us that someone is calling. "Traffic light turning red" is an event that signals that cars need to stop. Real world is full of events. Following are some of the commonly used events in Snap. You will find these blocks under the "Control" category.

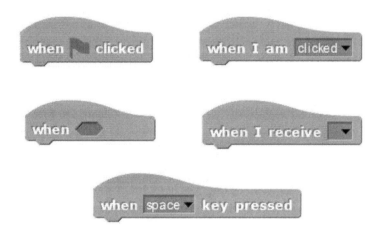

Every sprite in your program will have scripts to respond to the events that that sprite is interested in. For example, the paddle sprite in a game might respond to the "when up arrow key pressed" event by moving up a little as shown below:

We already understand several of these events such as "when green flag clicked" and "when key pressed". We will learn about rest of the event blocks later in this book.

Reset script:

Every sprite has a set of attributes (properties). We can call this set its "state".

- Position on the screen (X, Y)
- Orientation (Angle with North)
- Color (default value is 0)
- Size (default is 100%)
- Visibility (visible or invisible)
- Costume #
- Graphic effects

After we run scripts, one or more of these properties change. For example, see this script.

After running it, the sprite's location, direction, color, size, and visibility will all have changed. We will need to reset these back to the original values before we run this program again. This is done by the following script:

This is called a "reset script". By simply pressing the "r" key (or whichever key you use in your script) you can set the sprite properties to their original values.

Concurrency - running scripts in parallel:

We will try to understand the concept of concurrency (also known as "Parallelism") through some examples. Start with a program in which a sprite wants to move and talk at the same time. Can a single script do it? Try the following script in which we wish to have the sprite say hello while walking back and forth.

It doesn't quite work as expected, does it? This is where concurrency comes to help. Split this script into two scripts as shown below:

Now if you click on the Green flag, the sprite will continue moving non-stop and say hello every 3 seconds.

Concurrency basically means doing multiple actions at the same time. People like you and me are doing multiple things at the same time, all the time! For example, when we take a walk, we listen to music or talk on the phone, watch for road signs, react to a buzzing fly, and so on. All these actions happen concurrently.

Here is another Snap example:

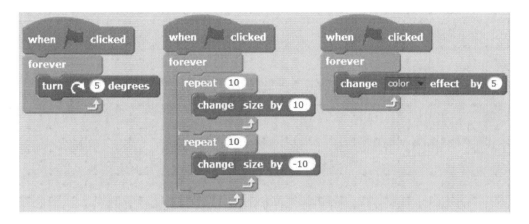

We have three scripts for the same sprite. The first script makes the sprite spin around itself. The second script changes its size continuously. And the third script changes its color continuously.

Because all three scripts start with the same signal, which is "Green Flag clicked", the sprite will appear as if it is performing these actions at the same time, that is, concurrently.

Review questions:

1. A sprite has a script as shown below.

If you make a duplicate of this script and click on the green flag again, what will happen?

    a. The sprite will run twice as fast since both scripts run at the same time.
    b. Nothing will happen because there is an error.
    c. Only one script will run because the two scripts are identical
    d. The sprite will not run in a straight line.

2. It is a good idea to write a separate RESET script which:
    a. Restarts Snap and opens your project file again
    b. Takes the sprite to its original position and direction
    c. Hides the sprite when the program is over
    d. Makes the sprite look in the East direction

3. See the following two scripts written for the Dog sprite:

S1:

S2:

Which of the following statements is true?
    a) The two scripts will do the exact same thing.
    b) The script S1 will move the Dog to the right.
    c) In script S1 the Dog moves left, but keeps facing right.
    d) In script S2 the Dog moves left, but keeps facing right.

Programming practice:

Note: Look up http://abhayjoshi.net/snap/book1/videos.htm to check out videos of sample solutions.

1. Make a bird sprite fly around the screen while changing size and color at the same time. Also have it make some sound every 5 seconds.

2. Make a ball roll from left to right of the screen. The ball appears at the left edge, rolls to the right, disappears across the right edge, and reappears again at the left edge.

Graphic Effects:

Snap provides a bunch of interesting graphic effects that you can use to make your animation very exciting. They are available under the "Looks" tab.

Color effect:
At the top of the list is color. Changing colors is of course very exciting, isn't it! The SET command simply sets the color to a specific value. There are about 200 different values you can use – from 0 to 200. The "CHANGE" command adds a number to your current color value. Why don't you experiment with these values and discover which value gives you which color?

This example script will show you 10 different colors in the range 0 to 200.

Ghost Effect:

Ghost effect has to do with disappearing slowly. So every time you increase the ghost value, the sprite will become fainter and fainter. At the value of 100 it will disappear completely.

If you want to make the sprite appear again, reduce value gradually back to 0.

This example script makes a sprite disappear and reappear – just like a ghost.

Fisheye Effect:

Fisheye effect is like pumping air into a balloon. Except in this case you pump air into your sprite. Just like the balloon bulges slowly as the air is pumped into it, your Sprite will bulge as you increase the FISHEYE value. There is no limit to how much air you can pump into your sprite.

To deflate, that is, to take the air out again, decrease the FISHEYE value gradually.

You can use a pair of repeat loops (as shown in the "ghost" effect above) to inflate a sprite and deflate it back to normal.

Whirl Effect:

WHIRL effect is about stirring your sprite with a stirrer as if it were a liquid. Or, think of your washing machine in which you wash clothes. The machine twists and turns the clothes, right?

Similarly, the WHIRL effect twists your sprite in either direction – right or left – depending on whether you increase the WHIRL value or decrease it.

You can use a bunch of repeat loops (as shown in the "ghost" effect above) to gradually twist a sprite clockwise and then twist it anticlockwise and then bring it back to normal.

Pixelate Effect:
Pixelate effect allows you to zoom into your sprite making it more grainy. You might have seen this type of effect in some of the older video games.

The maximum you can pixelate, that is, blur the sprite completely, is about 500. Beyond that the sprite becomes invisible. To bring it back to normal, reduce the PIXELATE value.

You can use a pair of repeat loops (as shown in the "ghost" effect above) to gradually zoom into a sprite and zoom back out.

Other Effects:
There are a few more effects such as *duplicate, negative, comic*, etc., that you can experiment with.

How to clear effects:
For any of these graphical effects that we saw so far, there are 2 simple ways to cancel the effect, and bring your sprite back to its normal appearance. The CLEAR GRAPHIC EFFECTS command cancels all graphical effects. If you want to just cancel one of the effects, use the SET command and set the value to 0.

Review questions:

1. Your sprite has undergone a lot of color change in your animation. So, in your reset script you would like to restore the sprite back to its original color. Which command will you use?

i.

ii.

iii.

    a) i only
    b) ii only
    c) iii only
    d) i or iii
    e) ii or iii

Programming practice:

3. Insert graphic effects in your earlier animation program or in a new animation.

Chapter 2.2: Keyboard Interaction and Conditionals

User interaction using keyboard:

One of the most interesting features of Snap is that it allows the user to interact with programs. Your programs need not be just animations that one has to watch, but, they can be interactive.

Snap provides the event block ![when key pressed] in which you can pick any key. Its purpose is similar to the block ![when clicked]. If you write a script under this event, it will run every time the user presses the specified key.

See these examples. In game programs arrow keys are typically used to move sprites. Here, the UP ARROW key runs a script in which the sprite moves 10 steps upwards.

Move the sprite when an arrow key is pressed.

Show help screen when "h" is pressed.

In the second example, the h key makes the sprite visible for a short time – this sprite could possibly be a "HELP" screen which pops up for a short time and then goes away.

Sensing touch:

In Snap, you can check if things are touching each other, and use that information in the conditional statements (such as IF, Wait until, Repeat until, etc.) which we will learn shortly. Here are the sensing conditions:

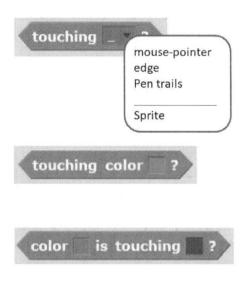

Sense if the sprite is touching the mouse pointer, any of the screen edges, pen drawing, or another sprite.

Sense if sprite is touching this color.

Sense if the first color (which must be part of the sprite) is touching the second color (outside the sprite)

An example of how sensing can be used in a conditional statement:

"Forever" is essential if you want to continuously watch for the touch.

See below to learn the IF command.

Conditional statements (IF):

In Computer Science there is a special type of question called the TRUE-FALSE question. For this type of question the answer can only be either TRUE or FALSE. For example, "Is it raining?" Or, "Are you going home?" Or, "Is 25 a square of

5?" The answer to all these questions is either TRUE or FALSE. There is no other possible answer.

Such questions are known as CONDITIONS.

Snap provides many such conditional questions and they are shown as diamond blocks. If you look under the SENSING and OPERATORS tabs, you will see several conditions. Here are some examples:

TOUCHING is a condition which basically is the question "Am I touching so and so?" There is another diamond block called TOUCHING COLOR which is the question "Am I touching this color?" The comparison operators compare numbers.

In real life, we use the TRUE-FALSE questions to take some action. For example, if the answer to the question "Is it raining?" is TRUE (or YES), we might decide to take the umbrella to school.

Similarly, in Snap we have a command called IF that we can use if a condition is TRUE. In the example shown below, if the sprite is TOUCHING another sprite called "fire", the sprite will say "Help! Help!" and then back off by 100 steps.

Conditional statements (IF-Else):

This is a variation of the IF command described above. See this example:

We want to move the sprite upward but not take it beyond the top edge. The condition in the above command is: "Is the sprite touching the edge?" If the answer is YES, the sprite doesn't move. If the answer is NO, the sprite moves up 5 steps.

So, the IF-Else command offers a fork in the process of decision-making.

Review questions:

1. See this script:

Which of the following statements is true?
   a) The SAY command will never run.
   b) The SAY command will run only if this sprite is not touching sprite1.
   c) The SAY command will run even if this sprite is touching sprite1.
   d) The SAY command will run only if this sprite is touching sprite1.

2. What will happen if we run the following script?

    a.   The sprite will move up

    b.   The sprite will move down

3. What will happen if you run the following script?

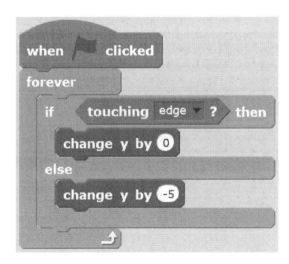

    a.   The sprite will not move.

    b.   The sprite will rise up and stop when it hits the top edge.

    c.   The sprite will fall down and stop when it hits the bottom edge.

    d.   The sprite will jump up and down continuously.

4. Are the following two scripts equivalent?

    a) Yes
    b) No

5. See the following two scripts S1 and S2.

Which of the following statements is true?

    a) These two scripts do the exact same thing.
    b) In script S1 the sprite bounces only on the left and right edges of the screen.
    c) In script S2 bouncing also happens if the sprite touches any other sprite.
    d) The scripts S1 and S2 will behave differently.

Programming practice:

Note: Look up http://abhayjoshi.net/snap/book1/videos.htm to check out videos of sample solutions.

1. Design a program in which a ball bounces up and down and is deflected by a paddle. The user should be able to move the paddle horizontally using the arrow keys.

2. Design a program in which there are several separate color circles (red, blue, green, etc.) on the screen. When the green flag is clicked an animal sprite starts following the mouse pointer and whenever it touches a circle its color becomes the same as the circle's. (Tips: (1) To make the animal sprite follow the pointer, consider using the "point towards" and "move" commands in a forever loop. (2) Consider using costumes for the animal.)

Stopping scripts:

The STOP commands (under the "Control" tab) allow us to stop Snap scripts in various ways.

The "STOP all" command stops all active scripts in your Snap project. For example, the script below checks if the allotted time has been used up, and if so, it stops the game. (Note: "time" is called a *variable*; we will learn about variables later in this book.)

The command "STOP this script" stops only the current script. In the adjoining script, a "prize" sprite waits until it touches "pacman". Since it has nothing else to do afterwards, it hides and stops its script.

Finally, the command "STOP other scripts in sprite" is useful when you want to only stop scripts of the current sprite. If you want to stop all scripts of the current sprite you would need to do as shown in the following hypothetical script:

This script waits until it hits any of the screen edges. Then it is supposed to stop all scripts of this sprite. It does that in 2 steps:

1. Stop other scripts.

2. Stop itself.

The following flavor of the STOP command could be used when you wish to stop everything else but continue doing some work – maybe it is some cleanup, or celebration of winning a game!

Finally, the following STOP command is used for custom blocks about which we will learn later in this book.

With the help of all the concepts learnt so far, we are now ready to take up a game project. Let's go for it!

Chapter 2.3: Project Helicopter

Description:

Using arrow keys fly a helicopter. Show the effect of gravity, i.e. if you don't do anything, the helicopter should automatically move down slowly. So, "Down" arrow key is not needed. The helicopter should be able to land on a helipad. Show moving clouds (just for fun). Have some indication, such as blinking lights or spinning fans, to indicate that the Helicopter engine is running.

Concepts used:

- User interaction (keyboard)
- Costumes
- IF-ELSE and sensing touch

Sprites:

1. Helicopter
2. Landing pad (can also be part of the stage)
3. Clouds

User Interaction:

- Green flag resets everything and starts the helicopter engine.
- SPACE BAR adds effect of gravity.
- Arrow keys (except "down") control the helicopter.

Additional requirements:

- The helicopter should land only if its landing gear touches the helipad.

The following image shows one possible implementation of this game.

Note: Look up http://abhayjoshi.net/snap/book1/videos.htm to check out videos of sample solutions.

Write in your Design book:

- A short description of your project
- Answer these questions:
  1. What did you learn?
  2. What was exciting?
  3. What was challenging?

Unit 3: Project Game of Maze

Often the hands will solve a mystery that the intellect has struggled with in vain.
– Carl Jung

Concepts learnt in this Unit

- User interaction using mouse pointer
- Conditionals (Wait until)
- Variables – numbers
- Variables as sliders
- Keyboard events (polling)
- User input (buttons)

Chapter 3.1: Mouse Interaction

User interaction using mouse pointer:

Here are the mouse event blocks that Snap provides. You are already quite familiar with the event WHEN GREEN FLAG CLICKED.

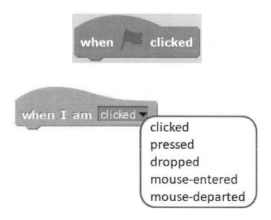

The next block includes a number of pointer events (as shown above):

1. Clicked – invokes a script when you click on that particular sprite. Imagine a button sprite, for example, that you could activate through such a script.

   In the script shown below, if you click on the bird sprite, the bird makes a "bird" sound and says "Chirp chirp".

2. Pressed – invokes a script as soon as you press the mouse button while it is over the sprite. It doesn't matter if you release the button sometime later; this script runs immediately after you have pressed the button.

3. Dropped – invokes a script after you drag the sprite to another place and drop it (i.e. after you release the mouse button).

4. Mouse-entered – invokes a script after the mouse pointer enters the sprite area (this happens irrespective of whether the mouse button is pressed or not).

5. Mouse-departed – invokes a script after the mouse pointer leaves the sprite area (this happens irrespective of whether the mouse button is pressed or not).

All these events, except "dropped", work for the stage also.

Another interesting thing you can do in Snap is that you can make a sprite follow the mouse pointer. The script shown below explains how this can be done. You make the sprite point towards the pointer and then take a small step.

If this is done continuously, the effect is to make the sprite follow the mouse pointer.

In fact, the same idea can also be used to make one sprite follow another.

User input (buttons):

It is common to have push-buttons (or rather click-buttons) to allow users to interact with programs. See the examples below in which I have imported the images from outside:

A click-button has the following properties:
- It is usually rectangular, oval, or circular.
- It has a label that describes what action it initiates.
- When you click on it, the specified action is performed in your program.

To implement a click-button:
- Get a button sprite (there are no built-in sprites, you will need to import from outside)

- Label it appropriately
- Use the "When sprite clicked" event to make the button active
- Send a broadcast message to whoever is supposed to carry out that action

Here is an example script for a "Draw" button:

When clicked, the button sprite sends a broadcast message to let everyone know that it was clicked. The actual drawing would be drawn by some other sprite when it receives this message. (In case you are wondering, you can draw all kinds of designs in Snap – we will learn all about it later in "Pen art".)

Review questions:

1. We have the following script written for the Alonzo sprite.

What will happen when we click on the Green flag?

a) Alonzo will follow the mouse pointer all the time.
b) Alonzo will point away from the mouse pointer all the time.
c) Alonzo will point towards the mouse pointer all the time.
d) Alonzo will move away from the mouse pointer all the time.

Programming practice:

Note: Look up http://abhayjoshi.net/snap/book1/videos.htm to check out videos of sample solutions.

1. Write a program in which the sprite jumps to the pointer whenever you click anywhere on the stage.

2. Write a program in which the sprite doesn't allow the mouse pointer to touch it. It runs away as soon as you move the pointer to it. The sprite stays inside the visible screen.

3. Write a program in which a wizard performs various types of magic for his audience. Provide a button for each magic, such that when you click on it, that particular magic is performed. For example, a button called "Frog" will turn a boy into a frog temporarily and then back to human form.

4. Create a solar system teaching aid in which an information bubble pops up when you take your pointer on top of any of the planets. For instance when you move the pointer over Jupiter, the bubble might say "Jupiter: the largest planet with 20+ moons." (Note: No clicking should be required.)

Chapter 3.2: Variables

Variables – numbers:

As you might know already, computers have a *temporary* memory called RAM. They use this memory to store information and do their work. For example, when you use a calculator program to make calculations, the computer stores the numbers you type in its memory. This memory is called "temporary memory" because the information goes away if you shut down the computer.

How does your program make use of this memory? That's where *variables* come in the picture. A *variable* is a location in this temporary memory, and each variable has a name. In Snap, you can create a variable by clicking on the button "Make a variable" under the "Variables" tab. Once you create a variable it becomes available to your program to store information.

When you no longer need a variable, you can delete it by clicking on "delete a variable".

The word "variable" means something that can vary or change, and indeed variables can contain any value. Snap provides commands that you can use in your scripts to store information in variables and then change it later.

The SET command stores a value in a variable. The value can be any number – negative or positive, whole, or decimal.

Later, you can change the value by using the command CHANGE. The CHANGE command adds the given number to the variable.

Let's look at an example of how variables can be used. Here we have a script for the game of maze. We have a variable called "Bonus points". In this script, this variable is incremented by 10 when a prize sprite touches the pacman.

Important: Always initialize number variables to some value (such as 0) at the beginning of the program.

Variables as sliders:

Let's use an example to understand this concept. Let's say we have defined a new variable called "speed". After creating the variable, it will show up on the screen as below:

If you right-click on this, you will see an option called "slider". Select this option. Now the variable will look like this:

It has become a slider variable. The user can drag the white knob and change the value of "speed" even while the program is running.

You (the programmer) can set lower and upper limits on this slider variable. Just right click once again and choose "slider min" and "slider max". For example, if you entered min=10 and max=40 the slider will only allow values in this range.

Review questions:

1. For which of the following cases would we need to use a variable?
   a) We want to make your sprite move forever, without ever stopping.
   b) We want to switch to the next costume when the spacebar is pressed.
   c) We want to keep track of the score in a game.
   d) For all of the above.

2. What is the value of "score" after we run this script?

   a) 100
   b) 50
   c) 150
   d) 0

Programming practice:

Note: Look up http://abhayjoshi.net/snap/book1/videos.htm to check out videos of sample solutions.

1. Write a program in which the sprite counts 1, 2, 3, ... infinity!

Chapter 3.3: Project Game of Maze

Before we look at the specification of this game, let's learn a couple of new ideas which would be useful in this project.

The "Wait until" command:

As we saw earlier, *conditions* are questions that only require a binary answer (yes/no, true/false). You are already familiar with how to use conditions in the IF command.

Sometimes in our programs, we want a sprite to just wait for some condition to become true. For example, here is a program in which a "prize" sprite is just sitting to be eaten by the *pacman* sprite. When *pacman* touches the prize, it is supposed to disappear.

WAIT UNTIL simply waits as long as the CONDITION is false. As soon as the condition becomes true, it stops waiting and the script moves to the next command.

Keyboard events (polling):

There are two ways to get keyboard input: one is using events (known in CS as "interrupt driven"), which we have already seen. The following is an event that signals a key-press and immediately runs the script. This script is called an "event handler".

The other way is called "polling" in which the program actively checks if a particular key is pressed.

If you want to check this continuously you must use a forever loop:

Polling (in a Forever loop) runs continuously taking CPU time, whereas event handlers do not take CPU time, because they sleep and are "woken up" when the event occurs. But, precisely for that reason, a tight loop like the one above is more responsive to user actions than the event-based approach. Another advantage of polling is that the program has full control on when to handle keyboard signals. When the program stops, polling also stops, whereas event handlers would run even if the program has stopped.

Another interesting advantage of polling is that you can combine multiple events using logic operators as shown below:

Maze Project Specification:

- Help an object, such as a pacman, travel thru a maze to reach a target.
- Sprite names must not be sprite1, sprite2, etc.
- Use the "h" key to show help, "Green flag" to set things up, and "Space bar" to start the game.
- Basic features:
    - A simple maze
    - Clearly visible "Start" and "Finish" locations
    - Prizes to eat along the way
    - Pacman moves with arrow keys or follows the pointer
    - Touching the walls of the maze makes pacman go back to Start
- Additional features:
    - Moving (or spinning) obstacles, when touched pacman goes back to Start
    - A monster follows pacman forever; when touched pacman goes back to Start
    - Use a variable to track prize points and penalties.
    - Timer

The following image shows one example implementation of this game.

Note: Look up http://abhayjoshi.net/snap/book1/videos.htm to check out videos of sample solutions.

Write in your Design book:

- A short description of your project
- Answer these questions:
  1. What did you learn?
  2. What was exciting?
  3. What was challenging?

Unit 4: Project Game of Bricks

In programming simplicity and clarity — in short: what mathematicians call "elegance" — are not a dispensable luxury, but a crucial matter that decides between success and failure.
— Edsger W. Dijkstra

Concepts learnt in this Unit:

- Relational operators (=, <, >)
- Variables as remote control
- Built-in variables - properties
- Motion - direction and bouncing

Chapter 4.1: Variables for Remote Control

Relational operators (=, <, >):

These operators compare two values and return true or false, depending on whether the comparison succeeded or failed. For example:

20 = 30 would return false

51 > -1 would return true, and so on.

These operators are typically used by conditional statements, such as, IF, Repeat until, etc.

We will take two variables "andy" and "tony" to represent ages of Andy and Tony, and see how the relational operators can be used to compare them:

Check if they are the same age.

Check if Andy is younger.

Check if Andy is older.

The "=" operator can also be used to compare strings:

Variables as remote control:

This concept is best explained through an example.

Let us say we have a spinning wheel as shown below:

If we wanted to change the speed of this wheel, we would need to change the input of the "turn" command. Instead of manually changing the number, we could use a variable in place of this input:

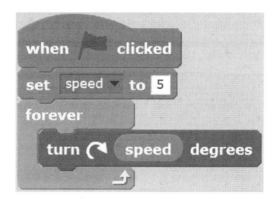

Now, whenever the variable "speed" changes, the spinning rate will also change immediately. So, the variable has become a "remote control" of the spinning wheel.

If you create button sprites labeled "Faster" and "Slower" with scripts as shown below, you will see how the remote control works:

Replacing fixed numbers (called "constants") with variables like this is also known as "parameterization".

Review questions:

1. What will the following script do?

a) Say "You win" if score is more than 100
b) Say "You win" if score is less than 100
c) Say "You win" if score is equal to or more than 100
d) Say "You win" if score is less than or equal to 100

2. The "glide" command has 3 inputs: time, x value, and y value. Below, we have a script that makes the sprite jump up and down. If we wanted to remotely control how fast the jump is, which input should we replace with a variable?

3.

    a. The "time" input
    b. The "x value" input
    c. The "y value" input
    d. All inputs

Programming exercise:

Note: Look up http://abhayjoshi.net/snap/book1/videos.htm to check out videos of sample solutions.

1. Write the above program to control a spinning wheel using variables. Include these buttons: start, stop, reverse, slow, and fast.

2. Modify your pong program (ball and single paddle) to add speed control. Add a slider variable to control the ball's speed. Count hits and misses.

Chapter 4.2: Built-in Reporter Variables and Bouncing

Reporter variables:

Snap comes with many useful variables that provide some information about the sprites, the program itself, or something else. We will call them *properties* to differentiate from variables that we create in the program.

For example, every sprite in your project has several properties; some examples are shown below. Their names clearly indicate what type of information they report. For example, "x position" reports the current X coordinate of the sprite.

Properties can be used just like any other variable. For example, the command below will make the sprite move left or right where X=0.

Snap also provides a way for one sprite to access information about other sprites through the following set of properties under the "Sensing" tab:

One big difference between your variables and properties is that properties are read-only; their values cannot be modified directly. For example, the "x position" property will change only when the sprite moves along the X axis.

Motion - direction and bouncing:

Generally speaking, whenever an object bounces off a flat surface, its incoming angle (with the surface) is equal to its outgoing angle. This is known as the "law of reflection".

Let's see how this works in Snap, where angles of sprites are given by the "direction" property. A sprite's direction is measured with respect to the North direction. So, if the sprite is facing north, *direction* = 0. If it's facing east, *direction* = 90, and so on.

If you make a ball sprite bounce around the screen and observe how its "direction" property is affected by bouncing, you will notice the following:

1. When a sprite bounces off a vertical edge (left or right), the sprite's direction changes only in sign. So, 30 becomes -30, -110 becomes 110, and so on.
2. When a sprite with initial direction A bounces off a horizontal edge (top or bottom), after bouncing the sprite's direction becomes 180-A.

So, depending on what type of surface (horizontal or vertical) the sprite is bouncing off, the calculation of *direction* would be different.

Review questions:

1. A sprite's "direction" property is 180. That means, the sprite is pointing towards:
    a. North
    b. South
    c. East
    d. West

2. Assuming the sprite is at the center (i.e. at x=0, y=0) what will the following script do?

    a. Move the sprite up-down 4 times.
    b. Move the sprite diagonally 4 times.
    c. Move the sprite in a square around the center.
    d. Move the sprite left-right 4 times.

3. What will the following script do?

a. Make the sprite go continuously where the mouse pointer is.
b. Make the sprite go once where the mouse pointer is and then remain there.
c. Make the sprite move left-right only as the mouse pointer moves.
d. Make the sprite move up-down only as the mouse pointer moves.

4. When a ball bounces around the screen, its "direction" property changes only in sign every time it hits an edge. True or False?

5. A sprite's direction or orientation is a built-in Snap variable. Which Snap command sets this variable?

a. `turn ↻ 15 degrees`

b. `point in direction 90 ▾`

c. `go to x: 0 y: 0`

d. `set x to 0`

Programming practice:

Note: Look up http://abhayjoshi.net/snap/book1/videos.htm to check out videos of sample solutions.

1. Write a program in which a bird flies in the sky continuously and a cat (or an animal of your choice) runs around on the ground exactly below the bird (in the hope to catch it).

2. Modify your Pong program that you wrote earlier and make the bouncing of the ball more realistic.

Chapter 4.3: Project Bricks

Project description:

This is a game you play with a ball and a flat paddle. A number of bricks are lined up at the top of the screen. As the ball bounces up and down you use the paddle to hit the bricks and score points. The ball must not touch the ground: after 3 such touches you lose the game. If you hit all the bricks you win the game. You can control the difficulty level of the game by changing the speed of the ball.

The following image will give you some more details of the game.

Brick sprites sit here until hit by the ball.

Controls speed of the ball.

Ball sprite moves up and down.

"Lives" shows number of remaining lives.

Paddle sprite moves left-right and makes the ball bounce.

Sprites:

- Ball and paddle
- Bricks (10 or more, any shape)
- Number of lives

User Interaction:

- Green flag to reset everything.
- Speed slider to set the speed of the ball.
- SPACE BAR to start the game.

Additional requirements:

- Paddle should only move horizontally, should follow the mouse pointer
- A "score" variable should count # of bricks hit
- Screens should declare win or loss

(Watch https://youtu.be/vm2LJy22HrU for a sample solution.)

Write in your Design book:

- A short description of your project
- Answer these questions:
  1. What did you learn?
  2. What was exciting?
  3. What was challenging?

Abhay B. Joshi

Unit 5: The Power of Variables

The secret of getting ahead is getting started.
– Mark Twain

Concepts learnt in this Unit

- Arithmetic operators (+, -, x, /) and expressions
- User input (ASK)
- String variables
- String operations (join, split, letter, length of)
- Variables – as counters
- Random numbers
- Algorithms
- STAMP - creating images
- Conditional looping (repeat until)

Chapter 5.1: Arithmetic and Strings

Arithmetic operators (+, -, x, /) and expressions:

Under the "Operators" tab of Snap, you will find the arithmetic operators:

All of us know these operators.

They can be used to create complex arithmetic expressions, such as, (20 + 3) x 5 (A – B) – ((C + D) / 10) where A, B, C, D are variables.

Equivalent Snap expressions for these are shown below:

Be careful with the precedence of operations when you combine these operators. For example, if you wanted to perform (10 + (20 x 5)) you need:

And not:

User input (ASK):

Sometimes you may want to ask the user to provide some textual information. The ASK command presents a text window and waits. The user can type his/her reply in this text window and press ENTER. Whatever has been typed is then saved in the "ANSWER" variable. See the script below in which the user types "25" in the text window.

Before running the script:

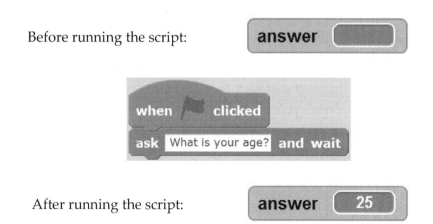

After running the script:

String variables:

The SET command (under "Variables") stores a value in a variable. Earlier we saw that the value can be any number – negative or positive, whole or decimal. The value can also be a string of characters. For example, you can create a variable called "Name" and store the value "John Luke Pickard" in this variable.

Obviously, the CHANGE command will not work for a string of characters.

Here is an example of how a string variable may be used. We have a variable called "Message". In it we first store the string "Hello World". Then, the SAY command takes that string from the variable "message" and prints it on the screen.

So, as you can see, you can use variables instead of actual values. When you refer to a variable in your script, the value stored inside that variable is used.

String variables can be modified by the "string operators" which we will consider next.

String operations:

A string is basically a sequence of alphanumeric letters:

The join operator allows you to concatenate two or more strings. In the script below, we combine 3 strings into a sentence:

The script asks you to type your name. If you type "George" the sprite will say "Hello George, how are you?" on the screen.

The "split" operator lets you split a string into two or more strings. The second input (let's call it the "separator") allows you to specify how the string should be split. The "separator" input can be one of the items in the drop-down list or it can be any string (with one or more letters). The resulting sub-strings are stored in a *list variable*. (We will study *list variables* later in this book.) For example, the script below will split by whitespace (i.e. any combination of space, line breaks, or tab characters) and create a list containing "one", "two", and "three".

The "letter" operator lets you get an individual letter of the given string:

The above script asks you to type your name. If you type "Melinda" the sprite will say "Your initial is: M" on the screen.

The "length" operator tells you how many letters there are in the string:

The above script asks you to type your name. If you type "Devon" the sprite will say "Your name has 5 letters".

Review questions:

1. What will the following expression give?

     a. -190
     b. 860
     c. -300
     d. 570

2. What will "score" equal after we run the script below?

3. If the variable x contains 2000, what will the following expression return?

4. Assume that the "answer" property contains 100 before we run the following script. What will the variable "x" contain after we run this script?

     a. Whatever the user types in response to the ASK command.
     b. 100
     c. Whatever the user types in response to ASK only if it's a number.
     d. Unknown value

Programming practice:

Note: Look up http://abhayjoshi.net/snap/book1/videos.htm to check out videos of sample solutions.

1. Write a simple calculator program that takes 2 numbers and performs basic arithmetic on them. Provide a button for each operation.

2. Write a program that converts Celsius to Fahrenheit and vice versa.

3. Ask for first, middle, last names, and then create full name and initials.

Chapter 5.2: Counters and Random Numbers

Variables – as counters:

In the script below, the variable "count" counts the number of repetitions:

It essentially counts from 1 to 10. This is called a *counter*.

This very simple idea of using variables as counters actually has several interesting applications. For example, you could use a counter while "indexing" a string – i.e. act as a pointer to the letter being read in the string as you scan the string. Counters are also useful in combinatorial problems – for instance, a problem in which you may ask for "all prime numbers in the range 100 to 500."

Programming practice:

Note: Look up http://abhayjoshi.net/snap/book1/videos.htm to check out videos of sample solutions.

1. Write a program that creates a comma-separated string of numbers. For example, if you provide 3, it will print 1,2,3; if you provide 5, it will print 1,2,3,4,5; and so on.

Random numbers:

Several outcomes (responses to events) in real life are unpredictable. Here are just a few examples:

```
Pick a ball out of a bag with your eyes closed.
Roll a die.
Toss a coin.
Decide what to wear to a party.
```

Outcomes of these acts are not completely random; they are random within some constraints. The outcome in each of the above is one of a set of possible outcomes. Coin toss involves 2 possible outcomes; retrieving a ball from a bag depends on the number of balls in the bag; roll of a die has 6 possible outcomes, and so on.

Snap offers a simple way to use randomness in programs through the following operator:

This operator returns a number from 1 to 10 – you can't predict what it will return. You can use any range (e.g. -100 to 100); the range can be in any order (e.g. 100 to -100); and it can even be a decimal range (e.g. 1.5 to 11.5).

The real key is to figure out how to use this simple operator to simulate the random events that you might want to use in your programs. For example, how would you simulate the roll of a die? Easy! use **pick random 1 to 6** since there are 6 possible outcomes.

Algorithms:

An *algorithm* is a step-by-step procedure that describes how a certain task can be performed. Strictly speaking, an algorithm has a formal structure (sometimes called the *pseudo-code*), which includes the initial and final states of the procedure, description of all inputs and the output, and so on. But, for the purpose of the programming projects in this book, we use algorithms rather loosely to create an informal *high-level description* of program steps, and help us in the process of creating the final Snap scripts.

Here is an algorithm for a real-life problem: Let's say we have 3 opaque bottles and one and only one of them contains salt. We need to find out which one. Let's assume all three bottles contain stuff that is eatable (i.e. not harmful to taste!).

Algorithm:
```
Arrange the 3 bottles in a row and name them A, B, and C.
Open A.
      If the stuff inside is powdery and white
            Taste some of it.
            If taste is salty
                  Declare that A is the salt bottle.
                  Stop work
            End-if
      End-if
Open B.
      If the stuff inside is powdery and white
            Taste some of it.
            If taste is salty
                  Declare that B is the salt bottle.
                  Stop work
            End-if
      End-if
Declare that C is the salt bottle. (No need to open and
taste because at least one bottle contains salt).
```

Here is an example for an arithmetic problem: Let's say we want to find out the largest among the given 3 integers.

Algorithm:
```
Given: P, Q, and R are 3 integers. "Temp" is a temporary variable.
Compare P and Q
      If P > Q
            Save P in Temp
      Else
            Save Q in Temp
      End-if
Compare R and Temp
      If R > Temp
            Save R in Temp
      End-if
Declare Temp as the largest number.
```

Here is an example from the world of Snap:

Algorithm to make a *rainfall*: (the sprite is a raindrop)

```
Forever:
   Go to a random point on the top edge
   Face downward
   Become visible
   Fall slowly to the bottom
   Become invisible
   Wait for a random amount of time
End-forever
```

Resulting Snap script:

Review questions:

1. What will the following script do to the Alonzo sprite?

   a) Alonzo will continuously turn, sometimes left sometimes right.
   b) Alonzo will not turn because random will always return 0.
   c) Alonzo will always turn clockwise because we have used the "Turn right" command.
   d) Alonzo's direction property will always remain between -10 and 10.

2. In the following script we have 3 variables x, y, z which get set to random numbers as shown below:

After clicking the Green flag, is it ever possible to have X=5, Y=5, Z=5?

   a) No, because random always returns a different number.
   b) Yes, because random may return 5 for all three.

3. See the script below. Which of the following letters is likely?

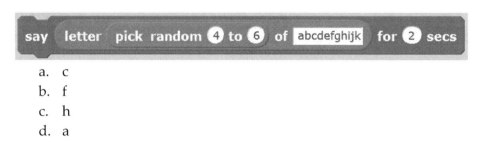

   a. c
   b. f
   c. h
   d. a

4. What range would you use in the RANDOM command to pick a month of the year?

5. If you wanted to use the "Go to x y" command to move your sprite such that it goes to any point at the top edge of the screen, what range would you use in the RANDOM command for the X value?

6. An algorithm is:
   a) A list of actions to perform, the order doesn't matter
   b) A sequence of conditional statements
   c) An ordered sequence of steps for carrying out a task
   d) Looping and conditions

7. Use a pencil and paper and follow the algorithm below. Which letter will be drawn?
   Position the pencil at the top right part of the page
   Draw a horizontal line
   From the middle point of this line draw a vertical line downwards, until it reaches the bottom part of the page
   a) L
   b) C
   c) T
   d) I

Programming practice:

Note: Look up http://abhayjoshi.net/snap/book1/videos.htm to check out videos of sample solutions.

2. Write a fortune-teller program (similar to the 8-ball toy) in which the fortune-teller can answer any yes/no type of question. For example, if you ask "Will I become the president?" the fortune-teller may answer "Maybe", or "Sure, why not!", or "No way!" etc. (Hint: The fortune-teller basically has a bag of ready answers; every time a question is asked he fishes out one of them.)

STAMP - creating images:

The STAMP command leaves an image of the sprite on the screen. See the example below:

The first one is actually an image, the second one is the sprite.

Although listed under the "Pen" tab, the STAMP command has no relation to the pen. So, to change the color of your image you must use the "change color effect" command. See the example below:

Once again, the first one is an image, the second one is the sprite.

To erase the images created by STAMP, use the CLEAR command.

Review questions:

8. Which of the following is true?
    a. The stamp command modifies the appearance of the sprite.
    b. The stamp command paints the sprite's image onto the stage.
    c. The image created by stamp gets cleared when the program stops.
    d. The image created by stamp can be moved using motion commands.

Programming practice:

Note: Look up http://abhayjoshi.net/snap/book1/videos.htm to check out videos of sample solutions.

3. Surprise flower: Upon every click of the pointer, a new flower comes up on the screen where you clicked. (Tip: Use multiple flower sprites, and then choose size and color randomly before every STAMP.)

4. Russian roulette: This program implements a simplified version of the Russian Roulette in casinos. There is a circle with each quadrant of a different solid color. A pointer is attached at the center of the circle. There are 4 buttons for each color. User clicks on one of these buttons, which causes the pointer to spin a random amount. If its tip stops in the color that the user picked, he makes money, else he loses.

Chapter 5.3: Project Falling Objects

Ok, it's time for another interesting project that will allow us to apply all the new ideas we learnt so far. But, before we discuss the project, let's just do one more new idea!

Conditional looping (repeat until):

In the simple looping covered earlier (Repeat and Forever), the repeat count is fixed beforehand. But, many times we may want to terminate the repetition based on a *condition*. For example, see the script below:

In this script, we want the user to enter his/her age. But, what if he/she enters a negative number? In order to ensure the age is a positive number, we need to continue asking the same question to the user until the user enters it correctly. "Repeat until" does exactly that: it asks the same question until age > 0.

Review questions:

1. How long will the following script run?

a. 5 seconds
b. 6 seconds
c. 0 seconds
d. forever

Programming project: Falling objects

In this game, some objects fall from the sky and the goal is for someone on the ground to catch as many as possible. All kinds of ideas are possible: catching gold coins, apples, raindrops, aliens, etc. The collecting sprite moves by following the mouse pointer or thru the left-right arrow keys.

Requirements:

- Use your own idea of falling objects in the sky.
- Use these concepts: conditional statements, broadcasting, sensing, user interaction, random.
- Sprite names must be as per the story.
- Objects must fall from random locations from the top so the catcher cannot predict where the next object will come from.
- Use variables to track points and/or # of attempts.
- Use the "h" key to show help, "Green flag" to set things up, and "Space bar" to start the game.

Here is a sample game screen in which the catcher catches gold coins.

Note: Look up http://abhayjoshi.net/snap/book1/videos.htm to check out videos of sample solutions.

Write in your Design book:

- A short description of your project
- Answer these questions:
  1. What did you learn?
  2. What was exciting?
  3. What was challenging?

Unit 6: Clones and Project Flappy Bird

We should continually be striving to transform every art into a science: in the process, we advance the art. – Donald Knuth

Concepts learnt in this Unit

- Object oriented programming (OOP)
- Clones
- Motion – piggybacking another object

Chapter 6.1: Clones

OOP - creating instances using clones:

OOP stands for "object oriented programming". In OOP, there is a concept of a "class", which defines the characteristics (i.e. properties and actions) of a collection of identical objects, and an object is an instance of that class. For example, "Tiger" could be a class with properties such as "height" and "weight" and actions such as "growling" and "hunting". And then an actual tiger that is 4 feet tall and 300 pound heavy would be an instance of this class. Loosely speaking, we can also think of a class as "parent" and objects as its progeny – children, grandchildren, etc.

Using this idea, a running program can have multiple instances of a class.

From Snap's perspective, every sprite can be viewed as a class which contains its own data (variables) and methods (scripts). And the idea of creating instances of a class is implemented using a feature called "clones". So, clones are basically identical copies of a sprite that exist only at run-time, that is, they are created by the program and they vanish when the program stops running.

The following command allows a sprite to create a clone of itself:

A sprite can create clones of other sprites too, as shown below:

A clone inherits (gets its own copy of) all scripts of its parent sprite except the ones that begin with the event "When Green Flag clicked". In addition, every clone, when it is created, runs (only once) scripts that start with the following event:

All clones are deleted when you stop the program using the STOP ALL command or by clicking the STOP button. Each clone may also delete itself using this command:

Although a clone is an identical copy of a sprite, it does not *share* the parent's private variables: instead, each clone gets its own copy of all private variables. For example, if the parent sprite has a private variable called "id", the clone would also have its own private variable called "id".

Similarly, the clone also gets its own copies of built-in sprite-specific Snap properties such as, *xposition* and *yposition*.

Snap provides another way to create clones, using the "reporter" block below:

The purpose of this block is to pass a newly created clone to another method (Snap block) as input. We won't be using this approach of creating clones in this book.

Review questions:

1. Let's say a sprite creates a clone. After creating the clone, if the parent's direction changes from 90 to 180, the clone's direction will also change to 180.
   a. True
   b. False

2. Let's say a sprite has the following two scripts.

After all clones have been created, if another sprite sends a broadcast message "message":
   a. Parent as well as all the 10 clones will say "Hello".
   b. Only the 10 clones will say "Hello".
   c. Only the parent sprite will say "Hello".
   d. Results are unpredictable because there is no "When I start as a clone" script.

Programming practice:

Note: Look up http://abhayjoshi.net/snap/book1/videos.htm to check out videos of sample solutions.

1. Write a program in which bubbles or balloons continuously pop up from the ground (from random locations) and float up to the top and then disappear. Use clones to create this multiplicity of bubbles (or balloons). Use a counter to track the number of "live" bubbles at any instant.

2. Modify the "falling object" program you wrote in a previous unit and use the idea of clones for the falling objects.
3. Modify your earlier "Bricks" game to use a single brick sprite which clones itself to create multiple bricks.

Chapter 6.2: Game of Flappy Bird

Piggyback motion:

When you design animation in Snap, there are instances when you want one sprite to "ride" another sprite, i.e. track another sprite's motion. For example, consider a horse-rider. Or consider an animation in which a person gets into a bus, drives to downtown, gets off and walks to his office. Such "riding" or "tracking" motion is called piggyback motion.

Achieving this piggyback effect is quite straightforward. You basically want one sprite (say sprite2) to track the motion of another sprite (say sprite1). Motion comprises the x and y coordinates and direction. The following properties can be used to access these values.

And sprite2 can use the following commands to continuously track the motion of sprite1.

In order to ensure sprite2 appears at the right place on top of sprite1, you may need to adjust the x and y values slightly by using the arithmetic operators.

Here is an example of sprite2 piggybacking sprite1:

"Flappy bird" Project Specification:

In this game project there is a flying bird, which "appears" to fly continuously to the left, and there are pairs of vertical bars (or pipes) with a small gap between them, that move from left to right. Each pair of pipes is exactly aligned vertically. The gap in each pair appears at a random height. The objective of the game is to make the bird move through the gap between the pipes. If the bird touches any of the pipes, the bird dies and the game is over. The bird can be moved upward/downward using the up/down arrow keys. The player is scored based on the number of pipes that the bird successfully passes through.

The following image shows the main screen of this game.

This setting decides how quickly the pipes move left to right.

Such a pair appears at regular intervals and glides from left to right.

This gap is at a different height for each pair.

The bird must pass through this gap.

This bird flies in place and can be moved up/down.

Design:

Use the following checkpoints and hints to design this program:

Checkpoint 1:
1. Get a flying bird facing west that flaps its wings.
   - Arrow keys will move it up and down
2. Get two vertical pipes ("upper" and "lower"):
   - Make them as tall as the screen
   - Make "upper" travel from the left edge to the right edge repeatedly, and use "score" variable to count repetitions
   - Set Y position of "upper" randomly
   - Align "lower" vertically with "upper" with a small gap between them and synchronize its motion with "upper".

3. Bird should sense touching both pipes.
   - If it touches any of the pipes, it falls down and game stops.

Checkpoint 2:
1. Add a "help" screen and start game with "space bar pressed" event
2. Add "Glide time" slider variable to control pipe speed.
3. Use clones to create "upper" and "lower" pipes:
   - "upper" parent will create a clone every few seconds (at random)
   - The clone will:
     i. Save its Y position in a variable.
     ii. Signal "lower" pipe and start moving
   - "lower" parent will create a clone when signaled by "upper"
   - The clone will calculate its Y position and start moving.

Write in your Design book:

- A short description of your project
- Answer these questions:
  1. What did you learn?
  2. What was exciting?
  3. What was challenging?

Unit 7: Procedures and Pen Art

A programmer who subconsciously views himself as an artist will enjoy what he does and will do it better. – Donald Knuth

Concepts learnt in this Unit

- Pen art
- Procedures
- Procedures with inputs

Chapter 7.1: Pen Art and Procedures

Pen commands:

Every sprite in Snap has a pen attached to it at the costume's center and is able to draw on the background. For the turtle costume the center is at its tip. The pen commands are listed under the "Pen" tab and they contain commands to put the pen down (after which the sprite will start drawing wherever it goes), pen up (after which the drawing will stop), set pen size, set pen color, and so on.

The actual drawing happens when the sprite moves using the motion commands. Using cleverly designed scripts, you can draw practically any type of geometric patterns. For example, the following script draws a pentagon:

The pen commands listed under the "Pen" tab help you perform various operations on the pen itself, such as set or change its size, color, and shade. Most of these commands are self-explanatory.

The **fill** command fills up the enclosed shape around the sprite with a color of the pen. See the following example:

Let's say we want to paint our favorite square with the color red.

We first draw the square using the following script:

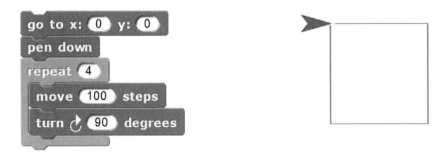

In order to paint this square, the turtle needs to first jump inside. Remember, it has to *jump*, which means it cannot draw a line while getting inside. Next, since we want to paint with RED, let's change the pen color to red. Finally, the actual painting job is performed by FILL. The following script performs these remaining tasks.

```
pen up
go to x: 50 y: -50
set pen color to
fill
```

The `pen trails` is an interesting *reporter* block that returns whatever the pen has drawn on the screen as a *costume*. You can save it in your list of costumes as shown below:

This instruction adds the current pen drawing into your list of costumes. This sequence is handy if you want to create a costume that looks like a complicated geometric design which is harder to *draw* by hand but easier to *program*!

Refer to the book *Pen Art for Scratch Programmers* written by the same author for a more detailed treatment of Snap's Pen capability and for numerous interesting programming problems.

Procedures:

A Snap *instruction* consists of a combination of one or more command blocks that we drag and drop in the script area, and which is then run by Snap when we click on it. For example, the following is an instruction which evaluates the expression 20*30 and shows 600 on the screen.

```
say 20 x 30 for 2 secs
```

A Snap instruction, like the one above, always carries out a specific, well-defined, and repeatable task. If you look carefully, you will notice that the instruction above contains the keyword "SAY" and the symbol "x" (for multiplication). Each of these words or symbols is called a Snap *procedure*. In other words, every Snap instruction consists of one or more Snap procedures.

A *procedure* is like a recipe of how to do something. For example, the MOVE command is a procedure that knows how to move a sprite. Several Snap blocks are thus individual procedures that carry out specific tasks.

Snap allows you to define your own procedures. At the bottom of every tab, is a button labeled "Make a block." You can also right-click in the script area and then choose "Make a block" from the menu. A dialog appears in which you can specify the name and type of the procedure. "Command" is a procedure without a return value and "Reporter" is a procedure that has a return value (and is also known as a "function"). "Predicate" is a reporter procedure that reports Boolean (true or false) values. We will not use the "predicate" type in this book.

The following picture shows that we are creating a new "command" procedure called "Greeting".

We have selected the "Looks" category (palette) for this new block.

When you click Ok, you see this dialog box:

Below the hat block "Greeting" you create a script by attaching existing Snap command blocks. This is what I created:

Clicking "OK" gives us a new procedure called "Greeting" in the "Looks" palette. You can use it in any script. For example:

Review questions:

1. What will the following script draw?

  a. Straight line
  b. Three parallel lines
  c. Equilateral triangle
  d. Incomplete square with 3 sides

2. What will the following script draw?

a. A series of equal size dots.

b. A series of dots of increasing size.

c. A series of dots of decreasing size.

d. A straight line

3. See the Snap command below. What is it?

a. An instruction

b. A procedure

c. Neither instruction nor procedure

d. Both instruction and procedure

4. The following script shows the definition of a new procedure called "jump". How can I use this new procedure in my Snap program?

a. By clicking anywhere on this definition

b. By sending a broadcast "jump"

c. By using the new block **Jump** in my script

d. By saving this definition in a separate project

Programming practice:

Note: Look up http://abhayjoshi.net/snap/book1/videos.htm to check out videos of sample solutions.

1. Write programs that draw the following patterns using repetition. **Hint**: Each design involves a repeating pattern. Once you identify the basic pattern, you can just use the REPEAT command.

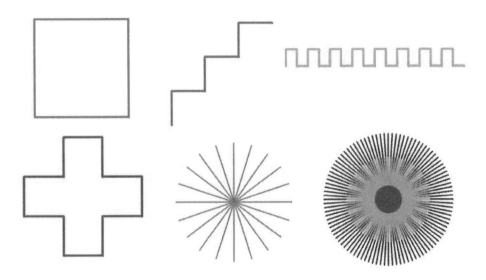

2. Using pen commands (including FILL) and the idea of looping (repetition), see if you can draw the following designs:

Chapter 7.2: Procedures with Inputs

Procedures with inputs:

The behavior of many procedures depends on how they are invoked. It depends on the *input* supplied. So, move ○ steps can do its job only when you tell it *how many* steps to move. Or, wait ○ secs command needs to know *how many* seconds to wait.

Snap allows you to define new custom procedures which take input. Right-click the new block "Jump" (which we defined earlier) and click "edit". You will see the block editor again.

We will add to "Jump" a *number* input labeled as "height". The label has no importance really, other than giving a descriptive name to the input.

Click the + sign to add an input.

You will see this input editor:

Type the name "height". Click the small arrow to choose your input type. In our case, the type is *number*. After clicking OK, you will see the following:

Now, the input is useful only if it is actually used in the procedure. You can drag the new input and drop it wherever appropriate in your sequence of commands. This is how our final "jump" procedure will look:

Note that we have to use the "multiply" operator in the second "change y" command to make the change negative.

If I use this new procedure in a script, say, as , the sprite will jump up and down by 100 steps.

Abstraction:

Abstraction is an interesting concept which means capturing a (relatively) complex idea into a single word (or phrase), image, map, audio clip, etc. Even in our day-to-day life we assign words to complex concepts or ideas. For example, "pedestrian" is an abstraction for *a person walking on a footpath*. Once we assign such words to ideas, we refer to the ideas simply thru those words.

Similarly, your new Snap procedure "Jump" is the abstraction for the idea of moving a sprite some distance up and down. Defining a new word which has a specific meaning is called abstraction.

Review questions:

1. Every Snap procedure requires input. True or False?
2. You can define a new Snap procedure that takes more than one input. True or False?
3. A sprite has a new procedure called "Square" as shown below. Which of the following is true?

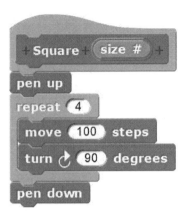

a. It will draw a square as big as the input "size".
b. It will not draw anything.
c. It will draw a square of size 100.
d. It will not draw a square but a set of 4 connected lines.

Programming practice:

1. Using procedure blocks that use input, draw the following shapes. **Hint**: Design your basic shape to accept inputs for size and color.

Chapter 7.3: Going in Circles

Drawing a circle:

A circle is drawn when the pen moves and turns continuously. So the following script would draw a circle of length (circumference) 360.

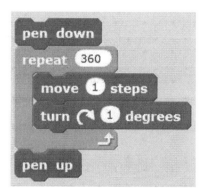

In reality, this script does not draw a circle; it draws a polygon with 360 sides each of length 1. But, for all practical purposes it looks like a circle. In fact, if you experiment a bit, you will discover that polygons of even less number of sides (say 180 or 100) also look like circles on the screen. But, remember that the total of all turns must always be 360 degrees.

Next, we can use the following formula that relates diameter of a circle to its circumference and come up with a Snap procedure to draw a circle of the given diameter.

Diameter = Circumference / 3.14159

So, "circle 50" will draw a circle of diameter 50; "circle 150" will draw a circle of diameter 150; "circle 200" will draw a circle of diameter 200; and so on.

Snap Turbo mode:

Every motion command in Snap takes a very short but finite time. This time actually helps in creating smooth animation because we can break down a long jump into multiple smaller jumps and then the series of jumps creates the impression that the sprite is moving smoothly.

For example, the script below makes the sprite turn slowly around itself.

But, this delay can be problematic for some other occasions. For example, if you are drawing a complicated drawing, say a spiral, the number of moves is quite large and so, the cumulative delay can make the drawing really slow. For such purposes, you can practically eliminate the delay by using Snap's "turbo" mode. Suddenly you will notice that your drawing has become much quicker.

Using "true" as input would turn the mode ON, and using "false" would turn it OFF. With turbo mode on, the following two scripts will be identical in behavior.

Review questions:

1. The following script is expected to draw a polygon of 180 edges. How much should the input to the "Turn" command be?

    a. 1
    b. 2
    c. 4
    d. 180

Programming practice:

1. Using the "circle" procedure block defined above, draw the following shapes.

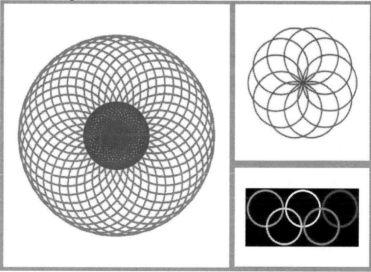

Chapter 7.4: Project Traffic Light

Description:

Draw (using pen, NOT paint editor) a traffic light as shown and animate it, i.e. make the lights go ON and OFF at regular intervals.

Add a two-way multi-lane highway and show one or more moving cars that move in each direction continuously but obey the traffic light, i.e. they slow down when the light is amber, stop when it is red, and move when it is green.

Additional requirements:

- As mentioned, the traffic light is not a sprite, but is drawn by the program using pen commands.
- Define the following procedures:
  - o "Fdcircle" procedure will draw a filled circle of the given diameter. The caller will choose the color.
  - o "Frectangle" procedure will draw a filled rectangle of the given height and width. The caller will choose the color.
  - o "Traffic.Light" will draw the full traffic light. It will take the diameter of each light as input and calculate all other dimensions accordingly.
- Create two separate versions of the program:
  - o In one, use only "broadcasting" to coordinate the interaction between the traffic light and the moving cars.
  - o In the other, use only "variables" to coordinate the interaction between the traffic light and the moving cars.
- Optional: Have a separate traffic light for each direction.

Unit 8: Additional CS Concepts

All you need in this life is ignorance and confidence, and then success is sure.
– Mark Twain

In this Unit we discuss a few additional concepts some of which have already been used in assignments and projects discussed earlier in this book, and some that would be helpful to you to write more challenging Snap programs. If you are looking for interesting and challenging problems to apply these concepts, please refer to the projects listed in the book "Advanced Scratch Programming" by the same author.

Procedures with return values:

What do we mean by "returning" a value? Let's consider a couple of examples. The Snap blocks "pick random" or "join" not only perform some well-defined function, but also *return* something. For instance, "pick random" *returns* a number, "join" *returns* a string. In CS lingo, such procedures that *return* a value are called "Functions". In Snap, they are called "reporters". Snap provides the block **report** to allow a procedure to return a value.

So far we have only created procedures that do something but don't return anything. They are similar to Snap blocks such as "move" and "turn" which similarly do not return anything.

Let us now learn how to create our own *reporters*. Let us say we want to create a reporter "max" that takes two numbers as input and returns the bigger one of the two.

The following picture shows how to create a reporter procedure "max":

The following script shows the definition of this new block called "max".

As you can see, it takes n1 and n2 as input and returns the bigger of the two.

Try running the following commands to verify that "max" works correctly:

Recursion:

The idea of recursion is a property of procedures. Simply stated, a recursive procedure calls itself. For example, the following procedure is recursive:

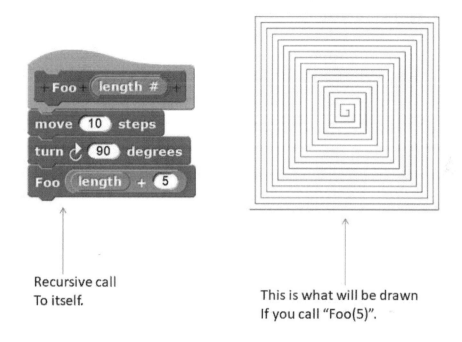

Recursive call
To itself.

This is what will be drawn
If you call "Foo(5)".

If you call this procedure, say by using Foo 5, it will draw a rectangular spiral forever; it will never stop because it will call itself indefinitely. What you will have is a program that runs forever!

Writing a program that never terminates is interesting but not very convenient. We would like to write recursive programs that do interesting things and terminate (i.e. stop) when their job is done. The Snap command stop this block will stop the currently running procedure and return to the calling procedure (or script). Thus, the infinite recursion will be broken.

Here is a modified recursive procedure that will not run forever:

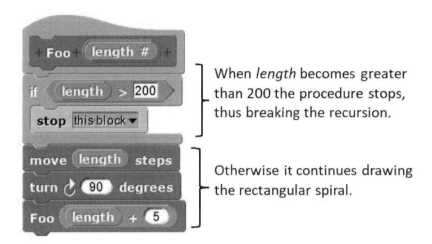

When *length* becomes greater than 200 the procedure stops, thus breaking the recursion.

Otherwise it continues drawing the rectangular spiral.

There is another, more general, way to make recursion finite, that is, make it stop after some time. We can simply decide how deep the recursion should go. See the modified Foo procedure below:

Here, let's assume *level* = 1 when we call Foo. It becomes 2 when Foo is called the 2nd time. It becomes 3 when Foo is called the 3rd time, and so on. "IF" will cause this recursive chain to terminate when *level* becomes 51.

Programming practice:

1. We used recursion above to draw a rectangular spiral. Modify your script to draw the following recursive patterns. As indicated, you just need to modify the turning angle.

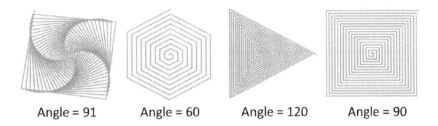

Angle = 91   Angle = 60   Angle = 120   Angle = 90

2. Refer to the chapter on "Recursion" in Logo Programming Part 2 and try to do the programming assignments given in that chapter.

3. Write a program to compute the factorial of the given positive integer. For example, factorial of 3 is 3x2; factorial of 5 is 5x4x3x2, and so on. (Hint: Consider using recursive procedure that uses the ⬛report⬛ block.)

List variables:

A list variable is a type of variable that stores multiple pieces of information: words, numbers, or sentences. In fact, a Snap list can contains even command blocks, scripts, and other lists.

To create a new list you use the reporter block ⬛list⬛◀▶ and assign it to a variable. Click the little left-right arrows to add more items to the list.

The above command creates a list containing one, 2, three, and 4 and saves it in the variable "mylist".

We can then use the following commands to manipulate the list. Let's imagine that we have a list variable called "fruits".

add grape **to** fruits   Add a new member at the end of the list

delete 1▼ **of** fruits   Delete the first item

insert thing **at** 1▼ of fruits   Insert a new member in the list (before
1
last
random
                     the given location)

item 1▼ of fruits   Get a member of the list
1
last
random

replace item 1▼ of fruits **with** banana   Replace by a new member
1
last
random

length of fruits   Get the size of the list

mylist **contains** papaya   Does the list contain the given fruit?
                                    This condition can be used in an IF statement.

Here is an example script that shows how the members of a list can be listed:

say I·have·these·fruits·in·the·bag: **for** 2 **secs**
set i▼ **to** 1
repeat length of fruits
     say item i of fruits **for** 2 **secs**
     change i▼ **by** 1

The following condition checks if the given item is present in the list:

146

```
if (fruits contains apple)
    say [I don't need to see a doctor!] for (2) secs
```

Programming practice:

Note: Look up http://abhayjoshi.net/snap/book1/videos.htm to check out videos of sample solutions.

4. Convert a sentence into individual words and then say it in the reverse order. For example, if the user gives "My name is Buddy" the program should say "Buddy is name My".

Logic operators (AND, OR, NOT):

Conditions, i.e. questions that return yes/no or true/false, can be combined using these logic operators, also known as "Boolean" operators. For example, in the script below, the sprite will say "We must be in heaven!" only if the temperature is in the range 60 to 90.

The best way to understand how the logic operators work is to construct "truth tables" as shown below.

The AND operator

Condition 1	Condition 2	Combined effect (output)
False	False	False
False	True	False
True	False	False
True	True	True

As you can see, the output is true only when *both* conditions are true.

The OR operator
See this example:

This script checks if you are pressing any key or clicking the mouse pointer.

Condition 1	Condition 2	Combined effect (output)
False	False	False
False	True	True
True	False	True
True	True	True

As you can see, the output is true when *at least one* condition is true.

The NOT operator
See this example:

NOT negates the given condition. So for a NOT expression to be True, the condition must be False. In the script above, the sprite will move towards the mouse pointer continuously but stop moving when it is touching the pointer.

Condition	Combined effect (output)
False	True
True	False

As you can see, the output is the exact opposite of the input.

Snap provides another interesting Boolean operator as shown below:

The value toggles between "true" and "false" when you click on the white circle. So, this operator always returns "true" or "false" as indicated. This could be useful, for example, if you have a *reporter* (a block that returns a value) that needs to return true or false. See the example below:

This reporter returns true if the sprite size is > 100, otherwise false.

Programming practice:

Note: Look up http://abhayjoshi.net/snap/book1/videos.htm to check out videos of sample solutions.

5. When the mouse pointer touches your cat sprite, it meows. It meows only once after touching. If you remove the pointer away and touch again, it meows again.

Conditional statements (nested IF):

The IF (and the IF-Else) command can be used in many variations. One variation called "nested IF" is shown below. Nested IF means having one IF command inside another.

This script is for a digital clock. It adds a minute to the time.

If the total minutes become 60, that's counted as an hour and counting of minutes starts again from 0.

If the total hours become 24, counting starts again from 0.

Mapping random numbers to a set of things:

Sometimes you want to pick something from a collection of things, which is not necessarily an ordered list of numbers. For example, you want to pick a color from the set of 4 colors: green, red, blue, and yellow. How would you do that using the random operator?

Well, the first step is to realize that the collection contains 4 items. So we should use 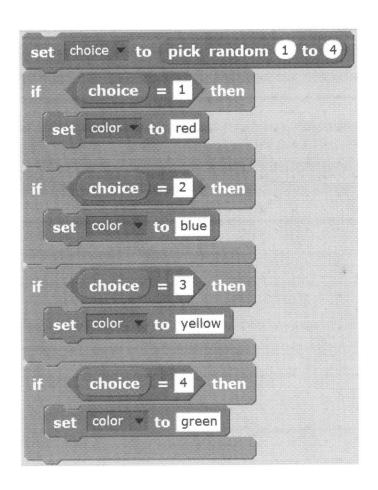 to pick from 4 numbers. Next, we can map each number to a color: so, 1 could map to red, 2 to blue, 3 to yellow, and 4 to green. Then, depending on what *pick random* returned, you would know which color to pick. Here is the script to show the entire scheme of things:

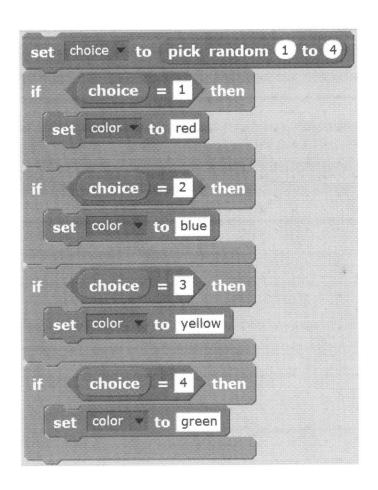

Mouse events (polling):

Similar to keyboard interaction, mouse signals are handled in two ways: one is called events (or "interrupt driven") as shown below:

The other is called "polling" as shown below:

If you want to check this continuously you must use a forever loop:

Note that the condition is "mouse down" and not "mouse click".

It is possible in the "polling" method that some mouse-downs might be missed if their timing does not match with when the IF command checks for the mouse-down. Also, polling (in a Forever loop) runs continuously taking CPU time, whereas event handlers do not take CPU time, because they sleep and are "woken up" when the event occurs. But the advantage of polling is that the program has full control on when to handle mouse signals. When the program stops, polling also stops, whereas event handlers would run even if the program has stopped.

Another interesting advantage of polling is that you can combine multiple events using logic operators as shown below:

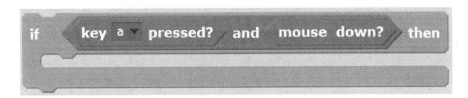

User input validation:

The ASK command allows the user to enter input, which could be words or numbers. For example, you might ask the user to enter his/her height. It is essential to ensure that the user enters a valid input, in this case, a valid height. Something like -50 or "abc" would not be a valid height.

The program must have a way to validate the user input, and if it is not valid, go back and ask again. The following example shows how this can be done:

Let's say we ask the use for his/her age. We assume that the age cannot be less than 1 or more than 100.

The loop continues to ask the same question until the user gives a valid answer.

Variables - local/global scope:

When you create a variable, you get the following dialog box:

Below the name, there are two options to select from: (1) For all sprites, and (2) For this sprite only. If you select the first option, you create a "global" variable, and if you select the second option, you create a "local" variable.

A global variable is visible to all sprites in your project. Any sprite can set it, change it, or use it. On the other hand, a local variable is visible only to this sprite (one in which you created it).

It is a good practice to decide the scope of each variable carefully, and make it "global" only if it is clearly going to be used by multiple sprites. For example, the "score" variable in a "pacman" game would be needed by multiple sprites (prizes, pacman, obstacles, etc.) so it should be "global".

A local variable, if displayed, uses a different notation. See below:

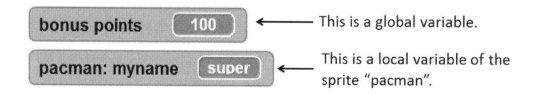

154

Using variables as gates:

There are occasions when the user must not be allowed to start playing the game until some setup is completed. For example, let's say your game starts when the SPACE key pressed. But, before pressing the SPACE key the user must set a few things, for example, slider variables. We can enforce this by using the concept of "using variables as gates". In the example below, we will use a variable called "setupdone" which will be False initially and True after setup is done.

 Set the variable to False initially.

 Start the game (by sending broadcast) only when set up is done. The variable will be set to True by whoever is in charge of setup.

Variables - as timer:
The combination of variables and the WAIT command can be used to implement a timer. See the script below:

The "time" variable is set in the beginning to whatever value you want to set for your game. The repeat loop then decrements it a second at a time until it becomes 0.

It may be confusing to see the "time" variable getting decremented and also being used in the REPEAT command. The REPEAT command uses its initial value (in this case 30) to decide the number of repetitions.

A more intuitive (and less confusing) way to do this might be:

Made in the USA
Middletown, DE
27 September 2020